I0622701

THE RISE AND FALL OF BOSTON PRIDE

THE RISE OF A MOVEMENT, THE FALL OF AN ORGANIZATION

DANIEL JOSEPH GONZALEZ

SHODAN PRESS

Library of Congress Control Number: 2024903240

Hardcover ISBN: 979-8-9900937-0-6

Paperback ISBN: 979-8-9900937-1-3

E-Book ISBN: 979-8-9900937-2-0

Book Cover Design by: Daniel Joseph Gonzalez

Book Cover Image: IStock https://www.istockphoto.com

Book Back Cover Image: IStock https://www.istockphoto.com

First edition 2025

"I guess we all have our own war stories, but they're meant to be shared. They have to be, because these stories, they're what bring us together, and they keep us alive."

—Sally
(Felicity 1x05 Spooked)

To Juliette and Nico

I hope your generation lives in a world without all the -isms and -obias.

ABOUT THE AUTHOR

Daniel Joseph Gonzalez, Ed.D, IMH-E is an early education expert working at Neighborhood Villages, an educational think tank in Boston, MA. Daniel lives in Massachusetts with his partner Tim and their dogs Bella and Harry.

Contents

INTRODUCTION

On July 9, 2021, the New Boston Pride Committee, Inc. announced they would shutdown. For twenty of the last fifty years, this committee ran Boston Pride, a celebration and protest to commemorate the Stonewall uprising in 1969 and is held alongside many other cities throughout the United States in June of each year since the riots. This shutdown surprised many, as the organization was suddenly shutting down, but to insiders, this was a long time coming. While it was not expected that the organization would shut down, advocates had been pushing for years to have substantive change occur, including having the president of Boston Pride resign.

In late June and early July 1969, a riot grew in the early hours at the Stonewall Inn, a gay bar run by the mafia in New York City, widely considered the start of the modern gay rights movement; riots and demonstrations had been occurring for at least a decade before the events of Stonewall. For instance, the Annual Reminder demonstrations were held in Philadelphia from 1965 to 1969, each July 4. Boston Pride and many other cities' demonstrations, rallies, and celebrations were built from events such as the Annual Reminder and the Stonewall riots.

The history of Boston Pride is vastly more complicated than just its messy 2021 shutdown. Boston Pride, before the New Boston Pride Committee's takeover in the late nineties, had been run by eight other committees and organizations. Decisions have been disorganized at times, often drawing conflict with the LGBTQ+ community in Boston. There have been moments where drag queens were not allowed to march during Boston Pride, complaints of commercialization long before corporations found it beneficial to use their money to push their products, lack of inclusion for hard-of-hearing participants, and culminating in charges of racism and anti-trans sentiments that lead to a boycott from prominent Boston and national organizations such as the GLBTQ Legal Advocates & Defenders (GLAD), and The Network/La Red.

Sitting along the Charles River, Boston was founded in 1620 and has been the site of battles, the first public park and public secondary school, the first annual marathon, and the first state to celebrate and have gay marriage. Much of the more recent LGBTQ+ history in Massachusetts has been held by various groups with no cohesive story. That is, until now. The book explores the events of LGBTQ+ people in Boston from 1970 through 2023. Using the lens of Pride, this explores the intricate ups and downs advocates faced in Boston. Pride is more than just a parade and a festival. It's the life of the LGBTQ+ community.

This book is written by decade and encompasses the history of Boston Pride and the pride movement throughout Boston. Chapter 1 covers 1970 through 1979, the beginnings of the pride movement in Boston, the decision-making process of early pride marches, and the formation of a split LGBTQ+ community. Chapter 2 explores the 1980s, the AIDS epidemic, the toll it had on the community in Boston, and how to create pride programming to match the sad moment of death in the LGBTQ+ community. Chapter 3 examines the LGBTQ+ community included in Boston's annual St. Patrick's Day parade, the wins, and untimely loss at the Supreme Court. It also investigates the financial health of Boston Pride in the late 90s, which led to a change in leadership for the parade and festival. Chapter 4 analyses the expansion of LGBTQ+ rights, including the first right to marry in the nation. This change affected corporations and allowed for more money to come to Pride. Under the leadership of Linda DeMarco, she developed a model that takes Boston Pride into the 21st century and longevity. Chapter 5 looks into 2015 to 2021 as the expansion of Pride's commercialization, the ignorance of Boston Pride to consider Black Lives Matter protest demands, and the lead-up to the dissolution of Boston Pride. Chapter 6 explores the final few days of the New Boston Pride Committee, Inc. through to their dissolution and the rise of Boston Pride 4 the People, a group that splintered off from Boston Pride and currently runs Pride events in Boston.

Like any telling of history, it is messy. Some material may be contradictory to what people remember. To be as transparent as possible, notes are included at the end of the book so you can check sources and gather information. Many sources come from newspaper reporting, which should be taken with a lens from when those articles were written. Along these lines, there may be language considered inappropriate today that was commonplace at the time. It has been left in for historical accuracy.

Because this is not just a history of Pride but also a journalistic endeavor, an ethics code was needed to drive this work. The code of ethics of the Society of Professional Journalists guided the decision-making of who and how participation in the project would proceed. Every effort was made to interview and allow persons who are mentioned to comment on the material about them. Many organizers declined to be interviewed, and this is referenced when appropriate. A significant list of notes and references is available at the end of the book. Quotes were gathered through newspapers, videos, audio recordings, and other forms presented to the public.

Boston Pride's 50+ year history is a powerful example of a group of people rising, demanding equality, and celebrating a community. It is a testament to all who celebrated, protested, and helped volunteer their time with Pride to have the longevity that Boston Pride has had. To all of them, we say thank you.

CHAPTER 1

THE RISE OF THE RAINBOW:
1969-1979

The events of the Stonewall riots are common knowledge today. Though not the first bar to be raided throughout the 1960s, the events in late June and early July 1969 have become legend. Physically or otherwise, the events of Stonewall were not the first time people fought back. What was different this time was that there was an activist infrastructure in place to spread Stonewall across the country. This structure, developed over twenty years, could communicate what had happened and capitalize on the events. And, with New York City as close to Boston, you'd have expected that word would have spread fast.

Boston, only a four-hour drive from New York City, appears to have been a mixed bag when it comes to knowledge of the immediate events of Stonewall. The *Boston Globe* did not mention the riot until 1972. The *New York Times* did write three articles on the raid; none made front-page news. As a result, outside of activist circles, the general public was largely unaware of the events.

Martha Shelley, one of the leaders of the New York chapter of the Daughters of Bilitis, walked with a group of activists interested in starting a chapter in Boston through Christopher Street on one of the nights of the riots.

> We saw these people, who looked younger than I was, throwing things at cops. One of the women turned to me and said, 'What is going on here?' I said, 'Oh, it's a riot. These things happen in New York all the time.'

Frank Morgan, a co-founder of the Homophile Union of Boston (HUB), heard about it in a July 1969 article from the New York Mattachine Society called "The Hairpin Drop Heard Around The World." Bill Conrad, a doorman at the Boston gay bar Sporter's, remembers,

> Sure, people were talking about [the uprising]; the place was buzzing about it. They'd walk up to each other and ask if their friends had heard about it.

Within six months, all the activist organizations throughout Boston were aware of theStonewall events. They chose to do something to commemorate the riot with a nudge from The Eastern Regional Conference of Homophile Organizations.

The Eastern Regional Conference of Homophile Organizations, a regional activist group on the East Coast, wrote a declaration in March 1970 to all LGBTQ+ organizations that the last Saturday in June should be held annually in remembrance of the riots. They called on all organizations and individuals who would like to demonstrate to do so. New York and San Francisco activists chose to hold a march and rally. Boston activists, many of whom were HUB members, decided to celebrate the first anniversary of Stonewall with a series of events and discussions, without a march or parade. John Mitzel, who organized 1971 Pride and who was later part of the Boston-Boise Committee, reminisced,

> After Stonewall happened in New York, the idea of doing a march in Boston was in the air, but we were the only radical gays in town; no one else was going to do it.

As a result, the first March did not happen in Boston until June 1971.

With the coordination of six organizations, a flyer was sent around the city by the Homophile Coordinating Council of Boston in early June 1970, a joint venture by the Daughters of Bilitis, Student Homophile League, Homophile Union of Boston, the Council on Religion and the Homosexual, and the Gay Liberation Front. This flyer spoke of Stonewall, known at the time as the Christopher Street Liberation, with a week-long series of events including a panel discussion, worship at the United Methodist in South Boston, and a seminar on the homosexual lifestyle.

Publicity around the events was sparse outside of the flyers. Activist Diana Putnam told the *Boston Phoenix* to "come out of your closet before they nail it shut." There was a quick mention of the week-long workshops by Tom Ellis of *WBZ*, and two of the organizers were interviewed by reporter Steve Schatz, but that was it. When asked about what there was to celebrate, Frank Morgan replied,

One night, the police just went too far...and the homosexual community rebelled –stood up, fought back, and said, 'No, you're not going to step on us any longer.' This is the first anniversary of that event, and it's what we're celebrating here in Boston this weekend.

The flyer and events did reach the Boston mayor's office. Mayor Kevin White pressured the Charles Street Meeting house to cancel a planned dance during Pride week. Advocates were unable to find another location in time for the dance.

A contingent from Boston traveled to New York City to celebrate the first anniversary of the riots under the banner "Christopher Street Gay LiberationDay 1970". John Mitzel, writing in his diary at the time, that he found it novel that the *New York Times* placed the rally in Central Park on the front page. The crowd was estimated at around 3,000 to 5,000. *Life Magazine* referred to 1971 as "the year that one liberation movement turned militant" due to the number of LGBTQ+ people standing up around the United States.

***

Organizing the first Pride march in Boston in June of 1971 began in a Fenway neighborhood apartment with only a few people in attendance. They included John Mitzel and Charley Shively, who considered themselves radicals for planning a protest march. Shively and Mitzel would go on to create the Fag Rag, a journal dedicated to post-Stonewall life as an LGBTQ+. There is some confusion on exactly when they began to prepare for June. Some sources say it started in the winter of 1971, while John Mitzel wrote that it took about a month of planning, distributing, coordinating, and completing, likely from May to June of 1971.

There was disagreement about what exactly they would be protesting about and how they would go about it. As planning progressed on a week-long series of events, culminating in a protest march, most of the planning committee representatives came from various gay organizations in Boston. This committee called themselves the United Front of Gay Organizations in Boston. Some representatives included Diane Travis, Reverend Magorah Kennedy, Dana Kaplan, and Laura McMurray. There was a sign painting party at Diane Travis's apartment for the March that would take place in late June. It also included three members of the Socialist Workers' Party (SWP). There was some curiosity as to the three's motivations as they were not part of any of the gay organizations, but it was felt that if they were willing to work on the March and were gay, they were welcome.

Suspicion grew as the planning meetings progressed, and the SWP members were there for other reasons. Part of this was because the Socialist Workers' Party had a policy of excluding openly gay members from its organization. Another was an incident a few days before Pride week. Two days before the start of Pride Week, the SWP sponsored a forum on gay liberation, implying that this was an official part of Pride Week. The rest of the committee was in the dark about this event and felt they were using it for their own purposes. This event, billed as promising to have speakers from the organized gay community, only had one speaker who was not associated with the SWP, and the speaker was not endorsed by the group of which they were a member.

The SWP would be a part of the early days of Boston Pride and other Prides around the country. In 1976, David Thorstad published documents from the Socialist Workers' Party showing that the leadership in the SWP was trying to understand how far along the LGBTQ+ movement was in the early 1970s and had conducted a"probe" of the community to know whether they would back the community at large as part of their movement. By 1973, this probe had ended, and the decision was that while the rank and file within the movement were okay, including homosexuality as part of their broader movement, there was much backlash from the leadership of the SWP to drop the issue. Throughout Prides of 1971 and 1972, you could see SWP members as part of the crowd marching with signs that say "Socialist Workers' Party."

Events for Pride 1971 included a worship service at St. John Evangelist Church, a session on gay relationships, a workshop on sexism, a dance at the Charles Street Meeting house, and the march on Saturday, the 26th of June. There was an agreement among the planning committee members that there would be no tape recordings or pictures at any of the workshops throughout the week as they did not want to discourage discussions among those present and felt that people might be dissuaded from participating if they knew they were being recorded or videotaped. At the Wednesday workshop on sexism, a member of the SWP told other committee members that a tape recorder was set up that there was someone from the MIT radio station, "Voices of Dissent," and upon further inquiry, that this was allowed by the SWP member.

A further conflict broke out on Friday night when SWP members were handing out a position paper on gay liberation called "The Militant" and wanting space in gay publications. During the event, many in the audience agreed through spontaneous and loud applause when a member of a women's group got up and detailed how the SWP attempted to subvert their independence. The SWP member on the planning committee got up and demanded equal time and was met with scorn and boos. This debate lasted throughout the event, and by the end of the event, disdain for the SWP was growing. John Mitzel felt that

> the SWP and its representatives have proven them-
> selves to be agents of the arbitrary and expedient pow-
> er-seeking that the gay movement has rejected.

These workshops had roughly 50 to 80 people at each.

***

Armed with yellow balloons with the word GAY, the first protest march in Boston of the Pride era took off on Saturday, June 26th, 1971. Assembled on the corner of Tremont and Boylston Streets, the roughly 150 participants walked arm and arm on the sidewalks towards four locations.

Rose Tavano recalled that first march.

> We were so afraid that first parade. We didn't know
> what the repercussions would be. People were not as
> accepting as they are today.

The March had a heavy police presence but did not have to get the required permits because it was on the sidewalk. Some sources state that less than 100 people marched; however, most state figures closer to 150.

Their first stop was Jacques, a gay bar in Bay Village. Reverend Magorah Kennedy read a list of demands fashioned by women patronizing the bar.

> Because we can't go anywhere else because, as gay women, we have been especially ghettoized here in Boston, and because the conditions at gay bars are by and large determined by the straight world, those in control know they can be as oppressive as they want. Jacques is terribly crowded and a fire hazard on weekends. Women entering the bar were subject to taunts by [straight] men, who not only [took] up badly needed room but also got their kicks leering and propositioning the women here. Sanitary conditions hardly exist at all. We are effectively ghettoized since dancing between members of the same sex and other behavior which the law deems to call lewd and lascivious are illegal.

It was noted by Boston activist Allen Young that

> it is not a mere coincidence that most of the attempts to make parades more grandiose are being made by men, while most of the demands for simplicity are coming from lesbians.

The following three locations targeted representatives who were concretely antigay, developing a more sober tone as they went along.

Boston Police Headquarters was next in the March. Committee member Dana Kaplan read the list of four demands. They included,

1. That all entrapment cases cease.

2. That vague laws, such as those against loitering, disorderly conduct, and lewd and lascivious behavior, not be used to harass homosexuals.

3. That the police provide protection, rather than harassment, in areas around gay bars.

4. And that the police meet with representatives of the homophile organizations to facilitate communication and implement the above demands.

Boston, like many other cities, was arresting members of the LGBTQ+ community. Gay bars were extorted and shut down regularly, culminating in the indictments of Boston Police officers in 1988.

The third stop of the route was in front of theMassachusetts State House. Laura McMurry, a Pride committee member, read the subsequent two demands.

1. That all the following laws pertaining to homosexuality be repealed, including Mass. Chapter 272,

sections 34 and 35, as well as the city ordinance against same-sex dancing together.

2.   That legislation be enacted to end discrimination against people in employment, housing, and in the use of public facilities because of their sexual orientation.

Chapter 272, section 34 states,

Whoever commits the abominable and detestable crime against nature, either with mankind or with a beast, shall be punished by imprisonment in the state prison for not more than twenty years.

Section 35 states,

Whoever commits any unnatural and lascivious act with another person shall be punished by a fine of not less than one hundred nor more than one thousand dollars or by imprisonment in the state prison for not more than five years or in jail or the house of correction for not more than two and one-half years.

Continuing to St. Paul's Cathedral on Tremont Street, the President of HUB, Richard York, read the last four demands.

1. That the church accepts qualified gay persons for ordination and other religious work.

2. That the church recognizes and blesses the love of homosexuals as it does for heterosexuals.

3. That the church lends its support to the reexamination of the institution of marriage and the family, which in its present form legally discriminates against homosexuals.

4. That the church lends its support to the reexamination of roles based on sex, with particular attention to the fact that its support of the sex roles has oppressed women and homosexuals.

After the march to the Cathedral, the marchers ended their rally on the Boston Common with a closet smashing, which was staged to have a sizeable brown closet. This closet was torn apart as marchers held hands chanting "Come out!" and an emerged person came out and embraced a portrayed lover. Later that night, at the dance held at the Charles Street Meeting house, people were met with a sheet cake to celebrate the demonstration's success and rally. This was something they could not do a year earlier due to pressure from the Mayor of Boston.

***

Unlike in the first two years, the 1972 Pride Week commenced with little of the challenges that preceded it. John Mitzel commented in a diary entry that because of the SWP "infiltration," there was some contention as to whether there still needed a Pride week in Boston. However, it did not hold up the planning or commencement of Pride activities. By May 30, planning was in full swing. A priority was put on having a good sound system, something that was missing the previous year, to help carry the words of the spokespeople.

A meeting on Joy Street on Beacon Hill at the start of Pride week got heated, with gay activists discussing what they would gain from doing more Pride events. Many felt that it had been three years since Stonewall, and they had not accomplished much. These same people were among those who marched five days later. One person who spoke up at this meeting was a young Barney Frank, who, while not out at the time, attended the event anyway. Years later, Frank came out, became a United States Congressman, and married his longtime partner James Reedy.

Events for Pride Week started on Saturday, June 17, with a work-shop on being gay and Jewish. Other seminars included gay people and the law, gay people verse institutions, specifically prisons and hospitals, and a get-together and talk about "transvestites and transexuals." There was also a youth mixer and a movie screening of *Maedchen in Uniform*, a 1930s German film with openly lesbian themes. Towards the end of the week, there was a dance, a parade, and a rally. The rally and march began a new Copley Square route and ended in the Boston Common. The march was still less on the festive side, especially compared with upcoming years, and with more dramatic displays rather than festivity or humor. Elaine Noble soon, in 1974, became the first elected official in the United States as a member of the Massachusetts State House of Representatives; remembers about that day,

> Well, the first gay pride parade that I didn't even know we had to have a permit. And the second one, which people say was the first, but it was really the second one. I went to City Hall and got a permit. And the guy behind the counter, the young kid, was a man named Peter Mead, who's now chairman of the board of Emerson College's trustees. And Peter was so freaked that a teacher at Emerson came to get a permit for a parade called Gay Pride that he nervously typed in Emerson College as the recipient of the parade. So the permit was mailed to the president of the college. So needless to say, I got this four page letter saying how I had jeopardized the nonprofit status. And of course, Barney helped me out with that, wrote a letter and told him to calm down.

There were protesters at the march. Most were peaceful however Brian McNaught, who would go on to be the second liaison between the Boston Mayor's office and the LGBTQ+ community in the 1980's, reminisced,

> People don't realize that in our early gay pride marches in Boston, anti-gay people threw cherry bombs into

> the parade. They thought we were just like goats that
> could be harassed as we were.

This harassment would subside after the first few Prides, but protesters would come and go throughout the history of the Boston Pride.

***

Over the subsequent two Pride parades, there was a focused disagreement about drag performers' inclusion. In 1973, Sylvia Sidney, a well-known Boston drag queen who performed throughout New England for forty years until her death in 1998, was crowned as the first Boston Queen of the Parade. Sidney wore a "plastic blue afro wig" and was driven by Elaine Noble. The Boston Ledger criticized Sidney's inclusion and the inclusion of drag queens.

> The parade was no more than an attention-getting
> device to kick off the week and draw attention to the
> gay community. But it was a poorly chosen tactic be-
> cause it merely underlined the image that many peo-
> ple have of a homosexual as a one-dimensional drag
> queen.

Skip Rosenthal designated himself as the Grand Marshal of the parade. He stated his philosophy on the controversy.

> These queens and dykes don't want none of your
> politics. If you want to get 'em out of the bars, you've
> got to give them a show, floats, banners, costumes.

The march of 1973 saw a new route yet again, but this route
stayed until 1978. The parade stretched over two city blocks and
was considerably longer than in past years. There was a parade order
for the first time in Boston Pride history, as there were now enough
participants to have a parade order. This time, a banner started off the
parade, followed by an organization that had no affiliation with the
gay community, the Braintree Braves Drum and Bugle Corps. This
surprised many because it comprised boys and girls under 12 years old.
Lois Johnson, who spent 20 years as president of the Boston chapter
of Daughters of Bilitis, reminisced,

> There was no gay band at the moment. That was in
> the 70s. So we went looking and looking and finally
> found a young band of kids from some suburban, I
> don't know, Quincy or wherever it was. And so we
> asked them. I don't think they particularly identified
> ourselves as a gay group or whoever made the con-
> tract. So they came. And they were little kids. They
> ranged from 10 to about maybe 12, 14. And they
> were so cute, their little hats were falling over their
> heads. But I think the leader, when he found out he
> was marching in a gay Pride, just about fainted on the
> spot. But they provided music. They got paid. And
> they marched with us. Poor little kids at the time, they

were finished because it was a long, long, long march route. And they would say, "We're exhausted."

Many in the community could be heard saying how much they enjoyed the parade, and a reporter overheard a lesbian stating,

This year's parade is much better than last year's. Last year, we didn't have a parade; we had a march.

There were chants along the route, including "2-4-6-8, come out before you suffocate" and "faggots and dykes unite." Though there were some chants, many fell on deaf ears and did not catch on, including "Come out, come out of the park wherever you are," which was given out along the route. Along the parade route, a group of pro-abortion demonstrators met with the participants at the Massachusetts State House. The two groups waved and cheered on each other as the parade strolled by. Between 300 and 500 people were estimated to have marched. There were brief speeches made by Elaine Noble, Bob Dow, Skip Rosenthal, and Barney Frank, and in a touching moment, the day was dedicated to Vincent Sacardi, a noted gay poet and contributor to Fag Rag, among other periodicals, who passed away earlier in 1972.

The rest of Pride week included several workshops, including "Where are we in the gay movement?", "High School Organizing" and three dances that the Gay Community Center Committee sponsored were held at the Charles Street Meeting House. There was also a play by Johnathan Katz called "Coming Out" that was performed at the Meeting House. One of the Pride events donated $256 to the victims of a fire in New Orleans. The fire was at the UpStairs Lounge, a New Orleans gay bar, and killed 29 people, injuring several others.

There was some concern over the safety of the community in 1973 after a variety of muggings and other physical altercations. A few weeks after Pride, there was a murder of a gay man and an assault of a lesbian woman. As a result of these events, many within the community started responding with meetings and the potential for self-defense courses and even a community awareness campaign. The mainstream media in Boston did not comment on these events but on a new newspaper called the *Gay Community News*. Copies of *Gay Community News* were handed out during Pride in Boston and, over the next two decades, became a staple for news about the LGBTQ+ community in Boston and beyond.

***

More disagreements happened over the 1974 Pride season. Much like last year, there was disagreement mainly by women, who complained that it was demeaning to have men in drag. Drag would ultimately become a staple of Pride celebrations throughout the United States and beyond. Still, there was also disagreement among the participants and committee members about whether or not it should be more celebratory and less political. Part of this was because organizers chose a Mardi Gras theme for Boston Pride. Disagreement over whether it should be political or celebratory would continue throughout the 50+ year history of Boston Pride, often pushing in one direction, then the other, and back again. The Boston Pride committee chairperson, Bernie Toale, noted,

> A political statement can be made in more than one
> way. You don't need black armbands.

Planning of Pride in 1974 was held mainly at the Gay Community News offices and began on April 16, with approximately 20 women and men in attendance. Many on the committee felt they wanted to do something different and that

> we are workshopping ourselves to death.

This was also the first time there was an elected chairperson for a Boston Pride year, with this first year being Bernie Toale and Lois Johnson. Many ideas floated in these meetings, including developing plans for an elephant, giant balloons, floats, and bands, making Pride more celebratory. Attendance at Pride was estimated to be between 600 and over 1500. The march was filled with red, pink, green, blue, and yellow balloons with "Gay Pride 1974" on them. Tin buttons that read "Stars and Dykes Forever" were being sold among the crowds.

One symbol that came out in 1974 was the lavender rhinoceros. Designed by Daniel Thaxton and Bernard "Bernie" Toale, it was designed at a time when there were few symbols for the LGBTQ+ community. Toale explained that

> the rhino is a much maligned and misunderstood an-
> imal and, in actuality, a gentle creature.

It was disseminated throughout Boston in two ways. First, in 1974, Pride, where a mascot was created on a flatbed and sent throughout the parade. Second, through an ad campaign with grant money to the

MBTA, which took filing a lawsuit to get placed. It was not until December 1974 that the ads were featured on subway cars. This symbol would last about a decade before being retired.

***

1975's weeklong events celebrating Pride included two picnics, a community group night, a discussion on the needs of the gay community, two raps, and, like other years, a parade. Elaine Noble addressed the participants at the Parkman Band Stand on the Boston Common with co-emcee Rita Mae Brown. It was decided at the first pride meeting for the 1975 Pride Week to have a bicentennial theme, using a float with the theme "200 years of Gay History." The community groups were designed as a chance for gays and lesbians to have a meeting or social event of their own throughout many communities in Boston. This concept originally started in 1974 but was expanded in 1975.

The parade was purposely led by women this year, with an estimated number of nearly 2000 people attending. Drag Queen Sylvia Sidney was dressed in a "hot pink" dress and on a truck float. Many participants were chanting, "2, 4, 6, 8 dykes and fags are really great," as well as "3, 5, 7, 9 lesbians are mighty fine." The only tension of note during the 1974 parade was when some marchers tried to divert the parade to Post Office Square. They wanted to rally support for Susan Saxe, a wanted lesbian for the death of a policeman during a bank robbery. This diversion failed as very few marchers chose to follow the outliers.

***

Pride took on a celebratory tone for another year in 1976 with a theme of "Gay Unity is Gay Strength," though Pride Committee members tried to keep the tone as serious as possible. This year, as well as in 1975, continued adopting a Pride name of New England Gay Pride. There were over 2,000 marchers at the parade, with a group of lesbian motorcycle riders leading the parade. Known as Dykes on Bikes, they were eventually renamed Moving Violations and are a staple of the parade today. This was the second year the Pride Committee chose not to allow bars or businesses to march in the parade. Lynn Rosen of the *Gay Community News* stated,

> It was felt that the parade was to reflect the gay community mainly as a political force since gays had suffered so many political setbacks this year.

The Massachusetts Democratic Party had failed to put gay rights on its platform, and Boston had been unable to pass several bills concerning gay civil rights. A Pride committee member summed it up, stating,

> I am firmly committed to being outrageous, but it is about time that middle-class America began to realize there are gay women as well as gay men and that the gay movement as a whole acknowledges the needs and rights of lesbians.

While the debate about what role businesses should have at Pride events went on for decades, businesses were eventually allowed back in and began sponsoring parts of Pride by the 1980s and continue to do so today. The Pride Committee tried to keep a birthday cake for the Gay Community News from being cut on the bandstand to keep the day relatively serious.

There was additional concern in 1976 about who was making the decisions and the rules of Boston Pride. Lynn Rosen made note of this in an issue of *Gay Community News*. Like the role businesses should play, this has continued to the present. There was very little media coverage of Pride, with no coverage from the Boston Globe or the Boston Herald. WCVB 5 camera operators were confronted about not filming the march. When they were asked why they were not covering it, they stated,

Channel 5 does too much gay coverage anyways.

WHDH 7 and WBZ 4 were noted as having some coverage.

Like the other years, Pride week included a variety of workshops. These included workshops on third-world women in prisons, third-world women in relation to third-world men, racism, an open forum at Boston City Hall, a workshop on gay liberation and radical politics, and sexism within the gay community. There were also several dances, neighborhood meetings, and a picnic after the parade.

***

The planning of 1977 commenced with roughly 40 people participating. John Mitzel was surprised at who was participating in the committee for 1977. He last worked on the 1973 Pride committee and noted that several were bar queens and the church people.

He felt that they and Joe Leo were attempting to take control of the committee. Joe Leo had grand ideas of placing the parade on the Esplanade with a banner reading "Gay Liberation through Jesus Christ." Mitzel had every intention of toning down Leo's rhetoric, pushing away the conventionality of past Pride, and pushing for political speakers again. He told a subcommittee that.

> I predicted it years ago: that everything with gay liberation that was up for sale would be snatched up by the mafia. All the rest would become health clinics and social services agencies.

When a member of the gay Catholic group "Dignity" stated that the banner idea was not so bad, Mitzel chose to vote down any speakers who were pushing for money, including religious groups. When the final selections were made, many of those voting were business community members, including bar managers and owners. The decision was to have Jacqui Mac as the Emcee, Ann Maguire and Charley Shively as keynote speakers, Elaine Noble and Barney Frank, as well as two members of the Boston Advocates for Human Rights Speak, Ken Withers and Peter Maroon.

Additional decisions that were made in 1977 included rejecting the term "gay rights" and instead using the term "gay pride." As a result, the theme became "Gay Pride, Celebration, Introspection". The committee stated to *Gay Community News* that

> We deliberately and purposely rejected Gay Rights as
> this year's name.

Estimates for the Pride parade were between 3,000 and 7,000 people. Again, like last year, lesbians began the parade and included many groups, including the gay Socialist's People's Party, the Boston Advocates for Human Rights, Heterosexuals for Gay Rights, and several gay religious organizations. Drag performer Sylvia Sidney was again part of the parade. Kate Gyllensvird spoke at the rally, stating,

> We have power in this movement. One reason is be-
> cause we do support each other. We have learned to
> see our individual lives as part of a common struggle
> against a heterosexist society which has always taught
> us to hate ourselves and to put ourselves down. There
> is growing Pride and respect in our movement which
> affects how we relate to each other and to the rest of
> society.

Nothing unusual happened at the parade or with the first several presenters at the rally; however, this was not the case when Charley Shively took to the podium.

Charley Shively, a professor at Boston State College, now known as UMass Boston, wearing his doctoral robes, took to the podium to condemn institutions that he blamed for the oppression of LGBTQ+ people. He held up a copy of his Ph.D. diploma from Harvard University and lit it on fire, stating it was "only worth burning." He then denounced the insurance companies and banks by lighting up his insurance card and a dollar bill. People began chanting "burn them" as he lit them on fire. Shively then took out the Massachusetts state sodomy laws, lighting them on fire as well. People continued to chant, getting more excited as they were burned. People were less sure about what would come next. Quoting the Bible's death sentence for homosexuals, Leviticus 20:13, he stated,

> If a man also lie with mankind, as he lieth with a woman, both of them have committed an abomination.

He took out a copy of the Bible and set it ablaze. What happened next was a combination of confusion, shouting, and a riotous situation. Some called, "You can't burn the bible," others, "Go to hell!" while others started to rush the stage. John Mitzel recalled,

> Charlie had asked me, prior to this event, he said, should I just take the pages of Leviticus and rip them out and throw them in? I said, Charlie, after you've burned all this other stuff, that would look tame. Just take the whole Bible and throw it in there, so the flames went off. And the Bible went in. And the fag-rag contingent was off over here, and right next to them was the dignity contingent, gay Catholics. And Brian McNaught was in town, and he was outraged.

In a newsletter for the gay Catholic group *Dignify*, they stated that the Bible was snatched out of the fire by people that were closest to the stage, and Shively was booed until he left the stage. The Bible was then stomped on to get rid of the fire. Mitzel continued,

> And this wound up in the news later that night,
> somehow the burning Bible got brushed out of the
> wok and wound up on the ground. And there's this
> very sweet old queen who I knew from the store. And
> he was stamping on the Bible to put the flames out.
> So when I went home at 11 o'clock during the news,
> there was this poor queen stamping on the Bible.

It was felt that this was giving ammunition to Anita Bryant, an anti-LGBTQ+ singer, and spokeswoman for the Florida Citrus Commission, to continue her work against the community. She was galvanizing people to come out across the country for anti-LGBTQ+ rights throughout 1977. Her "Save Our Children" campaign ultimately succeeded by repealing a discrimination ordinance in Miami-Dade County, Florida, but her reputation would never recover.

***

The events of 1977 Pride reverberated throughout the Boston community. There was equal condemnation and support for what Charley Shively had done with the Bible. *Gay Community News* was inundated with letters for weeks and directly impacted how 1978 Pride would go. Mitzel resumes,

> Anyway, that set off of brouhaha for the next six
> months of gay community news, believe me. Ministers writing, how dare you burn the Bible. And what
> he was doing was imitating William Lloyd Garrison

had burnt the Constitution, I believe, in Concord in 1852 or three or something. We talked about this. I can't remember all this. But that was a famous episode when, obviously, there was a protest to slavery in America, parts of America. Garrison had a big rally and he held up the Constitution. He lit it and burnt it. Well, that set them off, too. So it's nice that something still works every once in a while.

Decisions were made among the pride committee, now known as the Lesbian and Gay Pride Steering Committee, to exclude political and religious leaders from being speakers at the annual rally in the future. This made several committee members furious, including John Mitzel, who found it interesting that Ed Mede, a defendant in the Revere Sex Ring case and member of the Boston Boise Committee, could speak, but not Elaine Noble or Barney Frank. He felt that the committee was more concerned with their image rather than fighting back against oppressors. Mitzel would later change his mind, finding the day "sensational." The committee named Pride 1978 "We are Everywhere and We Will Be Free."

The typical week of activities turned into multiple weeks for the first time. The committee held a carnival a week before the parade at the Fenway to great fanfare, and on the day of the parade, they had a mobile child-care unit in place. Throughout the parade, several marchers and many elementary school teachers wore brown paper bags over their heads. They wanted to illustrate the dangers of coming out and working with young children. Sam Goldfarb, a participant in the march, remembers,

> I really didn't have the guts to go out on the street. I
> sort of stood, I went in and out of the street and then a
> lot of us who worked, I worked for public schools, you
> just couldn't risk that. So we put paper bags over our
> heads and gave ourselves some little eye things so we
> could see where we were walking. And that was very
> memorable because, and then when I went home that
> night I really felt good about being gay.

While more sedate than the year before, the committee did allow for letters from Barney Frank, Elaine Noble, Mel King, and Larry DiCara to be read to the crowd, estimated at roughly 7,000. A letter was also read from Susan Saxe, the incarcerated activist at the time of the parade. The stage was different than in the last year or two, with it being less "massive and cumbersome" and instead was a 20x20 platform from a pickup truck. Mitzel remembers that the crowd stretched the length of the Boston Common as the parade turned into the rally. Linda Carford from the Gay Business Association and Pride Committee; Alan Young, co-author of Out of the Closets: Voices of Gay Liberation; Leslie Cagen, a lesbian socialist and feminist; David Drolet of the Mass Caucus of Gay Legislation; and Kate Gyllensvard of Lavender Resistance spoke at the rally.

***

By 1979, Boston Pride had established itself as an annual event in Boston. There were concerns that it had become too white, middle-class, and for men. This is despite the significant increase in the number of lesbians attending Pride events. This won't be the last time this comes up when criticizing Boston Pride events, though, in this instance, the committee chose to act rather than purposely ignore the concerns and criticism. The committee meetings began in early March and met at the Harriet Tubman House in Roxbury, being chosen as a way to address the needs of working-class gays and lesbians and racial minorities. There was a gay town meeting on June 20 where Susan Rosen spoke. Susan was the executive director of the Homophile Community Health Service. She stated emphatically,

> No one has yet undertaken to access the special needs that gay people have for community services. In Boston, our little institutions have grown up in a helter-skelter fashion as individuals have perceived the importance of providing specialized counseling, medical or alcoholism treatment services for lesbians and gay men. Most of these services are far too small and too underfunded to reach out to the hundreds of thousands of gay people who live in the state. Even if the existing services in the gay community could make outreach to all the lesbians and gay men in Massachusetts, many other needs would remain unmet.

The rally for Boston Pride was broadcast in real-time for the first time this year. WBCN-FM and 89.9, a radio station run by the Massachusetts Institute of Technology, simulcast the rally and its speakers, including Ellie Johnson and Beverly Smith of the Combahee River Collective and Gail Bradley of Parents of Gays. There was a moment when Tia Cross, who was an independent speaker at the rally, raised the prospect that racism was rampant and was considered a white problem. There was some lingering frustration among people who attended the rally, but it calmed down quickly when compared to previous controversial statements made in years past. Taffy Comer, who was on the 1979 Pride committee, summed up the decade of Pride action by stating to the *Boston Globe*:

> We haven't given up fighting to be recognized. People think they don't know any gay people, but they've got to be amazed when they see a turnout like this. We're everywhere–in their offices, stores, and restaurants.

Indeed, the gay rights movement has come a long way from where it was a decade ago. However, the community was not prepared for what would come in the 1980s, a disease that was infecting and killing off members of the LGBTQ+ community in spades. The fight had only just begun to be recognized as equal.

CHAPTER 2

THE EPIDEMIC SIZED TRAGEDY: 1980-1989

1980 was a banner year in Boston. Boston celebrated its 350th anniversary and set a large celebration throughout the city. This celebration coincided with the annual Pride Week and was included in the official events. A task force of lesbians and gays created a guidebook to gay Boston and had it disseminated to people coming from all over to celebrate Boston. Included as part of Pride week was a slideshow by the newly formed History Project, which documents the history of the LGBTQ+ community in Boston. This newly formed organization would go on to host various events over the years, such as *Out of the Archives* and the *History Maker Awards*, and has the largest repository of documents about the LGBTQ+ community in Boston and of Boston Pride.

Other Pride events included an event for school workers, a health seminar for gay men, a juice bar for gay youth, a legal workshop, and a conversation on lesbian alcoholism. Picnics and bike rides added community building, and disability awareness events, such as the deaf awareness event, were added to the calendar to celebrate differences and commonalities.

Leading up to Pride week, co-chairs Beth Kelly and Tom Chiodo held 21 weekly meetings, and by the time of Pride week, with over 8,000 participants, nearly all LGBTQ+ organizations in Boston were represented in the Pride Parade. For the first time in Boston Pride history, men and women were equally represented on the Pride committee. The two weeks would be called "All Our Voices, All OurVisions" from June 14 through June 29. Beth Kelly declared to the *Boston Globe*,

> I want to affirm that there will never again be another season of silence for lesbians and gays in Boston or anywhere else! We cannot afford to let our differences divide us. Beatings, rapes and murders stand as violent and graphic reminders of how much we are hated and feared in a society which remains predominantly sexist and homophobic.

Tom Chiodo echoed the sentiment.

> This is the one time of the year when lesbians and gay men can really get together and celebrate the fact of our existence. This is a chance one a year for a certainly very diverse community to express their unity and uniqueness. We spend the year really struggling for our rights and this energizes us to continue to come out and to feel a part of the community.

What was not known at the time and would not be known en masse was a pandemic event that would disproportionally affect the LGBTQ+ community. 1980 and 1981 Pride events were oblivious to the fact that AIDS would become a defining feature of Pride as money and research were scarce during the Reagan administration. The AIDS discovery would not be discovered until after the Pride events on June 5, 1981, and it took more than a year before enough people in Boston knew about it to organize.

***

On June 3, 1981, it was announced that Robin McCormack, the first liaison between the Boston Mayor's office and the LGBTQ+ community, was let go of his position. The reason was budget cuts due to Proposition 2 ½, which limited property taxes and reduced city revenue. This did not sit well with events ongoing for Pride in Boston, and protests were planned as a result. A three-hour public meeting was held at the Boston Alliance for Gay and Lesbian Youth (BAGLY) offices for the community to understand what had happened and what the community would do next. Beth Kelly stated during the meeting,

> Gay and lesbian lives are cheap these days. The time has come to initiate a direct action of protest. It is assumed we can be silenced. We must make it clear that we will not give up our right.

A crowd gathered on June 16 at 4:30 pm as Robin exited for the last time and marched to the Parkman House, a mansion that Mayor

White frequently used to rally for the job to be saved. Signs stating "Gay Rights or Gay Riots" and "You want Gay Taxes/We Want Gay Liaison" were held throughout the rally. In a moment reminiscent of the Boston Tea Party, protesters threw tea bags onto the mansion's doorstep.

With Pride right around the corner, Mayor White did not want a repeat rally on the steps of Parkman House to happen during Pride's parade. The city of Boston filed a lawsuit to change the parade route away from Parkman House with only days to go before the June 20 parade. City attorney Kelan Derderian made the argument that the large crowd of the parade would put an undue strain on the Boston Police Department and disrupt business on Beacon Hill. The Pride attorneys, John Ward and Cindy Rizzo of the Gay and Lesbian Advocates and Defenders (GLAD), argued that Robin McCormack had met to finalize plans for the march on June 16, and there were no issues. With only 18 hours to spare, Judge Paul Connolly agreed with Pride organizers, stating that the constitutional rights of free expression must take precedence over business interests. The city of Boston appealed, but the ruling was sustained, and the parade went on as planned and without incident. Boston Police estimated the parade to have 12,000 people.

By August, the Mayor of Boston relented and decided to reinstate the liaison position to the LGBTQ+ community. However, this position would not include Robin McCormack, and the search began for the next liaison. Brian McNaught took over this position in June 1982 after some political wrangling between the advocates, the Mayor's office, and Elaine Noble.

***

Controversy comes with the job on the Pride Committee. Weeks before 1982's Pride events began, critics spoke out against the decision on Pride speakers at the rally. They felt that there was an imbalance of speakers who were active in the All-Peoples' Congress (APC), which was a nationwide coalition of organizations against Reagan's approach to cutbacks, war, and racism. Three of the seven speakers were of the APC and were initially chosen by a subcommittee of roughly five people with no connections to the APC. By the time it moved to the full committee for a vote, there was "almost a coup" by the 15-20 committee members who were also a part of the APC. The Pride committee tried to lessen the damage in the media by having Marshall Yates communicate to *Gay Community News* that

> [We] made no attempt to stack either the rally or the meetings. When we came in on the night that the speakers were voted in, a separate committee had already brought forth the decision of speakers.

Further, Pride Co-Chair Marsha Levine stated,

> People were concerned that a majority of the speakers did represent the All Peoples' Congress. However, the speakers were also representing as individuals a diversity in the community.

This controversy led to a change in how Boston Pride chose its speakers. The main suggestion was to use a system that "balances votes from individuals and organizations." This approach was used in Pride committees in San Francisco and New York City.

The speakers that were chosen for 1982 included David Scondras, who started the now Fenway Health and became a political figure as the first openly gay Boston City Council member in 1983, Eric Rofes, a Harvard graduate and gay activist and writer, Kate Silver, a member of BAGLY, Linda Gwizdak, a member of the APC among other organizations, Marshall Yates, activist and part of APC, Natasha Raymond, APC member, and Chris Madsen, who was a former reporter for the Christian Science Monitor who was fired for being a lesbian.

1982's Pride was Boston's 12th annual event. With a theme of "It's a Nice Day to be Out," attendance for the parade and rally was estimated between 13,000 and 14,000; however, police only estimated the foggy grey day at 5,000. The largest contingent in the 1982 parade was Boston Dignity, the Catholic gay group. Matt, a college counselor, explained the power of the parade.

> Everyone in the parade has thought twice about coming out and being spotted. If we manage to raise the number of people in the parade by 1,000, that means 1,000 more people are willing to take a chance.

After 1982's Pride events, Marsha Levine, co-chair of Boston Pride, reached out to other Pride committees and organizations to network and share information on how they were producing their prides. In October 1982, they met in Boston and formed the National Association of Lesbian and Gay Pride Coordinators. This group would eventually transform into today's InterPride, an organization that has banded together with Pride organizations worldwide to network.

***

In September of 1982, the Centers for Disease Control used the term "AIDS" for the first time. Acquired Immune Deficiency Syndrome replaced the term "GRID," which was Gay Related Immune Deficiency. While it would be years before President Reagan said the word, funding was not increasing enough to meet the need. Advocates throughout the United States pushed for more funds and outreach about this increasingly dangerous pandemic.

By the end of 1982, groups were forming in Boston to advocate for AIDS research and support. Bartenders in gay bars were given a seminar on how to talk to customers about AIDS, and the AIDS Action Committee was formed. What would come are Pride events centered around AIDS for years.

Before the start of Pride on June 16, 1983 called "Stepping Out With Pride", a town hall meeting was convened to give updated information on AIDS. Over 600 people attended the town hall, primarily gay men. Sponsored by the Boston Lesbian and Gay Political Alliance at Faneuil Hall, many questions and concerns were expressed, including how little the science community knew of the pandemic and about making sure that people with AIDS were not victimized, stigmatized, or isolated within and outside the LGBTQ+ community. A candlelight vigil proceeded the meeting, walking to the Massachusetts State House to demand increased funding for AIDS research.

At the rally for the 13th annual Pride several days later, speaker AmyHoffman expressed,

> In addition to the fear and horror I feel about the
> physical danger my gay brothers face, I'm worried

about our whole community and movement. We must resist the feeling that AIDS means this exploration; this path to liberation was wrong. This feeling of homophobia: haven't they always told us we are sick, sinful, and disposable people?

During the parade, you could see men and women standing by each other, pushing for AIDS research. Robin Tyler, who was a political activist, stated,

> Lesbian women are standing by gay men with AIDS. We take care of our own.

With over 18,000 people marching, a large contingent was part of the AIDS Action Committee, which held up a green banner that commemorated those lost to AIDS. Steven Levine of Cambridge commented,

> I'm just always amazed to look at all these people and realize that each of these people thought once they were the only ones [to be gay].

The concerns of AIDS were palpable. John Mitzel wrote,

> How many of us—myself potentially included—have just a few years left?

Indeed, many more people would die of AIDS throughout 1983. Places like San Francisco would open entire wards dedicated to AIDS patients, leading to more chaos among the LGBTQ+ community.

***

While some people considered the 14th annual Pride events more of the same, it was anything but. The Pride committee chose to add a few new events to the entertainment to mixed reviews. This was the first time an entire festival would be introduced, with a few surprises. First, they added a camel. Yes, a real camel for rides. There was a general feeling that the camel did not look or feel well and was bothered by all the loud noises. Second, they secured a hot air balloon to be used for rides. Unfortunately, due to mechanical problems, the balloon never left the ground.

Over 17,000 people participated in Pride events. For the first time, participants were asked for a one-dollar donation to attend the events to offset the day cost at Boston Common, as the committee had spent $26,000 on the parade and festival. This elicited controversy as many people felt that the charge depoliticized the event, as did another committee decision. The Pride committee chose to drop the rally concept and have a celebration to coincide with the "Unity and More in 1984" theme, which was used nationally. There were only two speakers at the event: Harry Hay, who was the founder of the Mattachine Society and an active supporter of the pedophile advocacy group, the North American Man/Boy Love Association (NAMBLA), and Ann Maguire, who was recently appointed as the Mayor's third liaison to the lesbian and gay community.

Harry Hay eloquently stated,

It is by our ever-increasing visibility not only in new application of law and social custom but indeed also in the Arts that we seduce and recruit the children. But because we have never shared with our friends and well-wishers in the grass-roots consensus of the American Community our vision as to who we are and what we might really be about, that usually kindly-disposed American Consensus has now no bottom line of informed opinion or shared experience concerning us by which to fend off this barrage of evil and scurrilous deceit parading as religion and holy writ.

The parade continued to be felt as a necessary part of Pride events. Gary Drescher, who was a graduate student at MIT at the time, said,

It's an important part in the fight against bigotry.

And Carol Cookson, a librarian from Nashua, New Hampshire, commented,

I'm gonna march for as long as my legs will carry me. I just wish there were more parents here. And I just wish society would accept gays.

Virginia Apuzzo, who was the executive director of the National Gay Task Force, felt,

> Because we are gay and lesbian, because we are black
> and white, rich and poor, young and aged, and dis-
> abled, because we are oppressed, the oppression that
> we must speak out against is all oppression. No matter
> how oppression may have led you to feel frustrated
> and beleaguered, you, individually, have the capacity
> to change this.

The AIDS Action Committee lined the sides of Charles Street, near the Boston Common, dressed in green t-shirts and large banners, greeting the celebrants as they entered the festival. It was a grim reminder that the Reagan Administration was not taking AIDS seriously and was allowing men and women to die.

***

With planning well underway for the 15th anniversary of Pride in Boston, it became clear by April that yet another unrest was about to take shape. The Pride committee hired Michael Wasserman to be a promotion consultant for the festival. Several committee members disagreed with the hiring, and co-chair Greg Dorian was ultimately removed. The disagreement over the $4,000 payment became a battle over a confidentiality clause and an open letter to the LGBTQ+community. *Boston Phoenix* reporter Ric Kahn asked Wasserman about the $4,000 amount, and he sent a letter to the committee stating that this violated a confidentiality clause in his contract with the committee.

Marsha Levine, co-chair of 1985's Pride, defended the decision to hire Wasserman and to accept the confidentiality clause as it is considered "standard business practice." She explained that the organization

> [conducts its affairs] according to the by-laws. Any affairs financial are not dealt within a political way.

An emergency meeting was held, and Vice President Greg Dorian was reprimanded, ousted as co-chair, and forced into a probationary period. Dorian felt two different parties were on the committee, one more celebratory and one more political.

After these incidents, the Pride Committee issued a press release promoting the power and history of Pride.

> It is of great importance to us that each year there is a day in June when we can come out onto the streets of Boston with our loved ones and friends – visibly gay and lesbian – 20,000+ strong. This day is a statement to the world and ourselves that we are impressive in number, rich in our diversity, and proud of who and what we are. Our allies have joined us at our gay/lesbian Pride Celebration. The signs they carry proclaim their support and respect for us. They have let us know that we are not alone in the struggle for our rights.

In May, the Massachusetts Department of Social Services (DSS) chose to take away two children from a gay foster couple, Don Babets and David Jean. They ended the contract after initially assuring the couple that the children would be allowed to stay. This came after Governor Michael Dukakis announced a new policy emphasizing "traditional family settings" for foster children, and the Massachusetts House passed a budget amendment prohibiting DSS from placing children with openly gay and lesbian families. Outrage grew throughout May and June over this policy decision that gays and lesbians could not be foster parents, and over 2,500 people demonstrated as a result.

By the time of Pride events, much of the controversy over funds for the festival had subsided, but not the fury over foster care. An estimated 20,000 to 27,000 people participated in Pride events. The 15th annual Pride celebration theme was "No Regrets!" and the parade was led for the first time by the newly formed Freedom Trail Marching Band. Other groups who marched in 1985 were the AIDS Action Committee, Gay and Lesbian Liberated Youth of the North Shore, Saints Collective, New Jewish Agenda, Amethyst Women, Gay and Lesbian Counseling Services, and District 65 United Auto Workers. To mixed results, people were again asked to donate to the Pride committee, this time voluntarily by funneling money through a wire fence.

Don Babets and David Jean were invited to speak at the festival. In their speech, they spoke of the devastation over the Governor's decision not to allow gays and lesbians to foster children.

> We know that the recent actions of the state government have caused a pain in all our souls that will not soon go away. A pain that gnaws at our very hearts and our efforts to build a more just society. We stand together today, all of us, with our dignity and our Pride intact. No matter what they take from us they cannot and will not strip us of our dignity.

Angela Bowen took to the stage after to continue the theme of foster parents. Angela received the Fannie Lou Hamer Award for her work for women of color and against racism.

> Much has already been said about the homophobic action of one particular man and the unprincipled reporter who began this witch hunt. So I won't repeat that. What I want to talk about is the potential solidarity this awful incident offers to us all. If some of us have felt alienated from one another, for whatever reasons, all the various factions of the gay and lesbian community can feel solidarity on this one issue, at least. As can all our principled straight friends, families and political allies.

The policy on foster parents would only change in the late 1990s.

Gil Gerald, the director of the National Coalition of Black Gays, also spoke at the event. While Gil did not talk about the foster care issue, he spoke about the concept that the LGBTQ+ community was considered as "different people" and it should be embraced. He spoke,

> Yes, over the next fifteen years, let us accept the challenge of being a "Different People." A "Different People" because we refuse to be mean spirited in an era when it is being officially sanctioned be our government, a "Different People" because we denied that rising poverty was a measure of progress and prosperity. A "Different People" because the work of molding our community has only just begun, and we have a unique

> opportunity to fashion our community in such a way
> that we have even more reasons to express and feel
> Pride.

By the end of 1985, the cause of AIDS was determined to be the Human Immunodeficiency Virus (HIV), though it would not be announced until 1986. The fight nationally for AIDS funding was continuing with events such as the death of actor Rock Hudson and when Ryan White, an Indiana teenager, contracted AIDS through contaminated blood products that were used to treat his hemophilia. He was refused entry to his middle school, and advocates flocked to protect his right to education. Ryan and his family chose to speak out for national attention to the need for AIDS education.

***

The Pride committee chose to ignore the people's will in 1986, though you would not have known it from their theme of "Forward Together." After much debate within the community, Foster care took over as the big issue for the second year, but the Pride committee chose to ignore the problem. There were no speakers on the issue, and the concept of plastering the State House with "Foster Equality" stickers by the Gay and Lesbian Defense Committee was dismissed, stating,

> [that it would be a] damper on the people in the pa-
> rade.

People felt drawn to the parade to support the issue of foster care for the LGBTQ+ community, with little comment on the issue from the Pride committee. Many of the 25,000 to 34,000 people who had come out for Pride in 1986 had also felt that there was a lack of urgency around AIDS with the Pride committee and that they were not addressing it at all. A compromise was eventually reached about the stickers by putting them on a drop cloth from a wall, but more was needed to satisfy the community. The Pride committee felt that placing stickers on the State House would hinder the gathering of permits for next year. There was an AIDS fundraiser after the parade for more research.

The Freedom Trail Marching Band again began the parade. The parade had the crowd roaring with laughter at times when a man pulled off his wig and took a bow. He then blew kisses into the gathering. A man threw red carnations atop a four-story building on Tremont Street into the audience. Catherine Lohr, one of the Pride organizers, affirmed,

> In 1970, it was an unauthorized event that 50 coura-
> geous people marched in. In 1975, it was up to 8,000
> people. Every year it gets a little bit bigger. We area
> community that is careful not to exclude anyone.
> That's why we have sign language translators for our
> speakers. The people here come in all shapes, sizes,
> and colors. We are tall, short, fat, thin, black, Greek.
> We are everything you find everywhere. This is a day
> of celebration for us. The day that you can safely go
> down the street in Boston with your mate only comes
> once a year.

When the list of speakers had been released, many found it unsatisfactory with the lack of diversity, and with two of the speakers, Ann Maguire and Elaine Noble, they found hearing the same old information and rallying cry as "dull" due to their overuse at past Pride events. The only speaker of color during the event was John Bush, a black gay activist, who spoke about the exclusivity of the LGBTQ+ community, especially within the bar scene. He cited incidents from bars that would require multiple forms of identification from people of color and lesbians.

***

There were a few firsts for Pride in 1987. This was the first year a flag raising occurred at Boston City Hall to mark Pride. This was also the first time that a flag commemorating Pride was flown from a municipal building in the United States. The flag had an emblem of a rhinoceros on a pink triangle. The flag would be replaced in the years to come with the one designed by Gilbert Baker and its offshoot designs. Committee member David Knauf commented on the flag design,

> The flag is symbolic; we picked a rhinoceros because
> it has a tough hide but is a peaceful animal unless
> provoked. This is our chance to come out and say
> we're proud but not completely happy.

Second, this was the first time that Boston Pride had a sponsor. In the future, this would become a staple of Boston Pride as it would be a resource for putting on more events during Pride.

The theme for Boston Pride this year was "Out for Good." The committee did consider a theme of "The Harder We're Hit, the Stronger We Get" but ultimately chose "Out for Good" as the theme. Governor Dukakis reiterated on June 12 that he had no intention of reversing the foster care policy he had implemented earlier in the 1980s. To respond to this, the Gay and Lesbian Defense Committee erected an effigy of the Governor in front of the Massachusetts State House and had people place Foster Equality stickers on it. Groups joined in the parade specifically to protest this policy. During the rally, David Scondras, a Boston City Council member, stated,

> By excluding homosexuals from foster parents, Dukakis is saying that there is something fundamentally bad about the character of lesbians and gay men. It would be just as bad if you said that blacks or Jews were the foster parents of last resort. It's really disturbing.

Mary Saucier sold anti-Dukakis stickers. She told the *Boston Globe*,

> My sexuality is not important. What's important is that he's discriminating against gays, lesbians, and single parents. I'm against any politician who ignores the rights of peaceful individuals.

Confusion and problems cropped up on the morning of the parade, festival, and rally—changes to the parade route due to construction in Copley Square confused parade participants. There were fights with hecklers, which led to several injuries, and EMTs dealt with the injured with contempt. Another group was booked to use the rally area at the same time as the rally. Police demanded that the Pride organizers be told that in 1988, Pride could only be held on a Sunday. Notwithstanding, the parade for 1987 went on with the United Fruit Co. entertaining on the parade route and Moving Violations leading the parade.

The rally did go on with several speakers, including Larry Kessler from the Boston Aids Action Committee, Kevin Berrill, who was the NGLTF Violence Project Coordinator, David Scondras, Katherine Triantifillou, and Robert Jackson, who was a Black Boston firefighter. Six hundred green balloons were released during Kessler's speech to remember the 600 people in Massachusetts who had passed away from AIDS over the last five years. Circling Boston was a plane hired by the Reproductive Rights Network with a banner that read "Sexual Freedom Now!" Police estimated that 30,000 people attended Pride in 1987, with the organizers estimating up to 40,000 participants.

***

Committee members for Pride in 1988 decided on a new format to receive advertisements, a guide booklet. This booklet, published by the Pride committee, would list all Pride events, interviews with special guests, and, most importantly, advertisements from businesses in and around Boston. They formatted it with a magazine feel and a glossy two-color cover. The booklet would be modified over the next twenty-five years with advertisements coming from more prominent national corporations and increasingly become more of a center stage for corporations than the material Pride would add to the booklet. Controversy over corporate spending on Pride will be debated over throughout the years. By 2019, over 45% of the pages of the *Boston Pride Guide* were ads.

Pride went off without much controversy. Themed "Rightfully Proud," the parade highlighted AIDS with ACT/UP Boston marching with a large black coffin and black balloons to protest the deaths that have been attributed to AIDS. The Freedom Train Band led the parade, followed by Moving Violations again. Several women chose to oppose the foster care ban by removing their shirts and placing foster equality stickers strategically over their nipples. Dennis Lewis, who marched in a white wedding dress, affirmed,

> It's part of who and what Pride Day is all about. If it's helping people to not be prejudiced, then I'll wear a dress. We wear business suits and ties every day just like everyone else does. Today I am wearing a dress, but I'm still the same man underneath.

Mass Act Out developed an ingenious game during the festival and rally. For only one dollar, you could throw an egg at a photograph of Governor Dukakis. Mass Act Out made a good amount of money that day. Lois Johnson reiterated the right for all of the LGBTQ+ community to exist, stating to the *Boston Globe*,

> It's tremendously important to have some celebration of our right to exist. Society is saying there is something wrong with you and we want to get rid of you and we will...I find it still euphoric to march. No matter what your problem or what your strength, there seems to be some organization being formed

> around that. The celebration of life at Pride is very
> important for the mental health and emotional health
> of gay people.

There were many speakers in 1988, including Elaine Noble, Robin Ochs of Boston's Bisexual Women's Network, John Manzon of the Alliance of Massachusetts Asian Lesbian and Gay Men, Barney Frank, Cindy Rizzo of Gay and Lesbian Advocates and Defenders, and John Bush of Men of All Colors Together. Barney Frank urged his listeners at the rally to support Dukakis for President, stating that his record on gay rights,

> ...may not be perfect. But we should be ready to vote
> for him, and the day after the election get ready to
> aggravate him to be better.

David Scondras accused the Democratic Party leaders of "insulting Jessie Jackson's Rainbow Coalition." He felt that gay issues should be placed on the party platform at the Democratic National Convention in August, though ultimately, it was not.

> They're seeing something they don't want to see today
> but they'd better get used to it, because we're here to
> stay.

Ultimately, Dukakis was defeated for President of the United States in November 1988.

***

The committee was pushed to include the word "bisexual" into the official Boston Pride name in 1989, but they resisted the call to incorporate it. Matthew Hayes, a committee member, explained,

> Bisexual was included in lesbian and gay.

He further explained that Pride did not have "an infinite name." Many ultimately disagreed with this decision as bisexual is distinct from the terms "lesbian" and "gay."

A record-setting 60,000 people attended Pride in 1989. Themed "A Generation of Pride," the parade started with the Boston Alliance of Gay and Lesbian Youth (BAGLY), followed by the Prime Timers, which was an organization of older men. The Daughters of Bilitlis shadowed close behind. The concept around having BAGLY first was due to a feeling that there was a loss of historical knowledge of the Stonewall riots 20 years earlier. Warren Blumenfeld summed it up,

> There are a lot of young people who have never heard
> of Stonewall; we are losing our history over a short
> period of time.

Janet Kyle of the Pride committee still felt the strength of Pride as a whole,

> This is about having the courage to step out and say you're not afraid. That you can be proud of what you are.

AIDS was still on the minds as they participated. Bill Chiantella of Project Care commented,

> Ten years ago, there wasn't the celebration of seeing a friend who's still alive, of looking across and seeing someone you know who has AIDS and feeling the joy that they are still here.

Debate still raged about whether or not Pride should be as celebratory, especially with HIV/AIDS still raging across the country. Philip Schwartz, a Fenway area sculptor, commented,

> The day should be changed a lot. Every AIDS death is an act of violence. I think there should be more political things and less of a celebration. I realize there needs to be a celebration as well, but it's not time to celebrate. I don't see what everybody has to be so happy about.

A Boston woman agreed.

> I think it's great fun, a great parade, but I don't think it's effective. It's too much of a show. I suppose just living your life is a more effective way.

David Scondras disagrees.

> Gay Pride Day sends a political message that's very
> clear. The gay community votes like a bloc, acts like
> a family, has financial resources, and there's a lot of
> political power there.

The community's political power would be realized in the next
decade through wins and losses, including winning the right to marry
in Massachusetts in 2003 and losing the right to be in the St. Patrick's
Day parade in 1995.

CHAPTER 3

PARADES AND FINANCES: 1990-1999

The 1990s were a time of expansion for Boston Pride, financial missteps by the committees running Pride, and a change leading to roughly 20 years of stability for Boston Pride come the turn of the century. The 90s were also a time when the movement felt it could move beyond the borders of Pride month and be present at the St. Patrick's Day parade, only to be pushed back by the United States Supreme Court when advocates lost a monumental case at the Supreme Court in 1995. What had become standard in Boston by the 1990s was that the Pride parade and festival had become a staple of events in June of each year. While not everyone was a fan of how Pride was being run, the LGBTQ+ community was being seen, out, and proud, in person and print.

***

For the first time in Boston Pride history, the organizers, in April of 1990, incorporated as a 501 (C) 3 nonprofit entity named Lavender Rhino, Inc. With this new organization in place, they could increase and accept money from various sources, such as grants and charitable donations from other organizations, and provide a receipt for charitable donations. Considering that the average turnout at Pride was 75,000 people, this status would allow for more programming and a more significant reach throughout Boston and beyond. This setup coincided with the 20th anniversary of Boston Pride events, rallies, parades, and celebrations.

1990's turnout exceeded 80,000 people. The foster parent issues of the late 1980s were still happening, and earlier in the year, State Representative Steve Pierce introduced legislation to ban foster parents who were LGBTQ+ entirely. Luckily, it was written in a way that made it unenforceable by the Massachusetts Attorney General.

Much to the surprise of many, Boston Mayor Ray Flynn spoke at the rally. Flynn's Chief of Police was standing next to him as he gave remarks stating that an uptick in violence towards the LGBTQ+ community "won't be tolerated." Steve Tierney of the Massachusetts Lesbian and Gay Political Caucus noted at the rally,

The real significance of a generation of struggle is entering the mainstream of American life. As a community, we have come out of the closet.

With AIDS still raging across Boston and the world, groups were still coming out to Pride in full force. At the rally, Neil Miller, author of *In Search of Gay America*, quantified,

> In the last several years, we have seen so many more people getting involved in the gay movement and politics, men and women. AIDS played a major role with

> so many lives affected, with more people – gay and
> straight – involving themselves.

Indeed, many more did. ACT-UP Boston and the People With AIDS Coalition were part of a larger contingent of AIDS activists at Pride in Boston in 1990. Youth made up a large contingent as well, with the Boston Alliance for Gay and Lesbian Youth (BAGLY) chanting, "Three-five-seven-nine, gay kids are mighty fine." Many parents of LGBTQ+ youth were also in attendance, and the Parents and Friends of Lesbians and Gays (PFLAG) received cheers from onlookers at the parade.

***

When Pride season began in 1991, AIDS research and funding from the U.S. Government and the states were still lacking the effort needed to come up with a viable treatment or cure. Act/Up Boston chose June to highlight the continuing issue with a three-day vigil at Massachusetts General Hospital. This was part of a more extensive 18-month campaign highlighting the government's continued need for urgency in creating any treatment or cure. It would take until 1995 before the first antiviral therapy with little to show aside from new detection methods. After the vigil, the activists joined the Boston Pride parade/march.

The theme of Pride this year was "Together in Pride," which was fitting due to the 20-plus years of Pride events that were bringing the community together, with estimates for 1991 attendees at 90,000. This would be the last time Pride in Boston would be below 100,000 participants. Mayor Flynn again chose to speak at the event, as did out Boston City Councilor David Scondras and Anne Sanders, the Human Rights Commissioner and formerly the Mayor's liaison to the LGBTQ+ community. The keynote was given by Urvashi Vaid, who worked at the National Gay and Lesbian Taskforce. Vaid previously worked for the American Civil Liberties Union as a staff attorney on the National Prison Project. She commanded the audience, proclaiming a link between the LGBTQ+ community and that of military demonstrations in Washington, DC, to celebrate the end of the first Gulf War.

> As we gather here today on the common, the streets of Washington are filled with another kind of demonstration. At a cost of $12 million so far, the federal government is putting on a national victory celebration. Tanks and guns are parading on Constitution Avenue. Military hardware on display. It is strangely perfect that the celebration of the patriarchy's gun power coincides with the gay and lesbian community's celebration of Pride throughout the country. It points out the difference between nationalism and liberation. Nationalism seeks conformity to the national interest; it says what counts is what the nation-state needs. [Liberation] seeks freedom. Its goal is to maximize individual choice. It thrives on difference and pluralism.

Gay Community News' Steve Karpf wrote an article just before Pride, speaking about the power and importance of Pride. He stated,

One common statement is that Pride is a positive opportunity for our community to speak to heterosexuals about who we are. The diversity of messages deliv-
ered during the Pride march-from El Comite Latino
y sus Amigos, Dykes on Bikes, Daughters of Bilitis,
and Gay Fathers, to name a few-is by itself a refusal to
be neatly categorized under a stereotypical or limited
definition of being queer.

***

Between the Pride celebrations of 1991 and 1992, activists were looking for other ways to be included. The other major yearly celebration
in Boston is the St. Patrick's Day parade. Held in South Boston in
March of each year, it was established in 1737 to honor Bostonians'
Irish heritage and the patron saint of Ireland, St. Patrick. Activists have
tried unsuccessfully to join the parade in the past and, after attempting
to join in 1992, chose to sue the parade organizers for entrance.

Political winds were beginning to change in Massachusetts, with
acceptance going up to an all-time high for the LGBTQ community.
Several politicians joined in to communicate the desire for the South
Boston Allied War Veterans Council to change their minds. Governor
Weld stated at a press conference that it is "wrong" to not include the
community in the parade. Barbara Kay of the Irish-American Gay,
Lesbian, and Bisexual Pride Committee stated

Denying our rights is discrimination under the law. We ask our elected officials to stand with us against this blatant act of discrimination.

In response, the Council stated through John Hurley,

[The group is bent on] coming into South Boston for the sole purpose of disrupting us.

He added that the gay group,

Would not guarantee they would act in a decent way. We didn't know what they would be up to during the march.

Mayor Flynn attempted to get the groups together to work out the issue as a similar issue had arisen in New York City. His work went to the sidelines, though, as the organizers ultimately denied the gay community access to the parade. Because the City of Boston contributes roughly $8,000 per year to the parade, LGBTQ+ organizers felt that the ban was unconstitutional because it was a public event. While the money was given, the St. Patrick's Day parade organizers contended that it was a private event. Sarah Wensch from the Civil Liberties Union of Massachusetts stated,

You can't turn people away from a public event based on a category like sexual orientation. It's almost a public forum with government involvement. To turn people away based on sexual orientation raises serious legal issues.

The Irish-American Gay, Lesbian, and Bisexual Pride Committee attempted to negotiate by limiting their role within the parade. This, too, was denied by the Allied War Veterans Council. The gay groups had no choice but to sue. An initial decision was made to allow gay groups to march in the parade. Judge Hiller Zobel granted a temporary restraining order against the parade organizers. He commented,

> A peaceable march is not a threat to the organizers of the parade, nor the city. The constitutional right to peacefully assemble and express the views with which large majorities disagree is paramount to discourse in a free society.

Barbara Kay commented after the ruling,

> This is a victory for everyone, not just gays and lesbians and bisexuals. We're talking about the rights of all minorities.

Due to the public fight over the parade, five non-LGBTQ+ groups chose to drop out of the St. Patrick's Day parade ahead of the parade, citing fears over safety. Twenty-five marchers marched in the 1992 St. Patrick's Day parade to threats and jeers from onlookers. Those threats were not acted on during the parade, which went on as it usually did. This would not be the last time, though, that the LGBTQ+ community would fight to get into the St. Patrick's Day parade. Mayor

Flynn vowed after the parade to support the bids of the community to join in future parades, stating,

> We're going to have a parade in Boston that is going to be inclusive, this is going to be open to anyone who wants to abide by the rules. That's the way it's going to be.

***

For the first time in Boston Pride history, attendance topped over 100,000 participants. This was fitting as their theme in 1992 was "Pride Equals Power: A Simple Matter of Justice." A significant route change occurred for the parade as police were concerned about Operation Rescue, an anti-abortion group, protesting outside an abortion clinic on Tremont Street. This would have directly been in the parade's path and may have caused issues. Ultimately, there were no incidents between the anti-abortion protestors and the parade. Another reason the parade route was changed was due to complaints by the Charles Street Merchant Association that they were losing business during the parade, though some merchants did not like the change and raised objections over the parade route change, arguing that this did not affect their businesses. Ellen Convisser, President of the Massachusetts Chapter of NOW, condemned the route change, stating,

> I think it's important that we show support for the clinic.

David LaFontaine, the lobbying director for the Coalition for Lesbian and Gay Rights, also condemned the change in route. This route, however, remained in effect during Pride in 1992. Some members of the LGBT community attended the protest to stage support for the clinic.

***

In December of 1992, the Massachusetts Commission Against Discrimination issued a preliminary finding that gays and lesbians in the Irish group who wished to continue to march in the coming 1993 St. Patrick's Day parade were being discriminated against and had filed a scheduled hearing on the matter between the group and the Veterans Council. In its wisdom, the Council chose a different course of action, legal action, to gain a preliminary injunction to prevent the Commission from conducting a hearing on the matter. The Honorable Hiller Zobel was handed the case and ruled in February 1993 that:

> The history of the parade shows it to be a secular event.

He noted that the St. Patrick's Day Parade had been a historically nonreligious, civil celebration "without theme" and that gay pride groups could not be barred from marching in the parade. Cathleen Finn, a member of the gay Irish group, wanted nothing more than tolerance and understanding from the Veterans Council.

> I really hope the church and civic and community leaders will show leadership around this and ba-

sically preach tolerance and really encourage people
to be tolerant and to understand we are part of the
Irish-American community.

The Council's lawyer, Chester Darling, blasted the ruling and assured its members that they would continue fighting for the right to discriminate at the St. Patrick's Day Parade.

We have state-compelled speech, that's what this is.
We will appeal as far as we can appeal.

With this being the second time gays were allowed to be in the parade, the judge set some ground rules. First, they could only have a maximum of 25 participants marching. Second, they provide no literature during the parade. Because this was only a preliminary injunction, like last year, the ruling only applied to the 1993 St. Patrick's Day Parade. The lawyers for the gay Irish group, Mary Bonauto, and Philip Cronin, said that they would press for a permanent ruling after the parade. Legal action would continue throughout the rest of 1993 and into 1994.

***

Boston Pride was under a new organization in 1993. Lavender Rhino, Inc. moved out of the way to The Pride Committee, Inc., run by Janet Kyle and Joe Martini, with committee members including former State Representative Elaine Noble. Noble noted that after polling the LGBTQ+ community before Pride, they wanted "less politics and more entertainment" as part of Boston Pride. The decision was to make a week of entertaining events under the theme "A Family of Pride." Kyle noted that

> The big difference this year is the weeklong celebration of gay community achievements, especially in the arts.

The newly formed group received over $47,000 in contributions for 1993.

Events for Pride Week included an arts festival, a literary showcase, a festival with Fenway Community Health, a movie on the Esplanade, and three dances. While most of the week was dedicated to fun and entertainment, a Pride town meeting on Tuesday, June 9, at Faneuil Hall was dedicated to politics and run by David Mixner, who was connected to the Clinton administration. The parade noticeably included more businesses, frustrating some other participants and the people watching the parade from the sidelines. This frustration would grow over the next few decades as the conversation over whether it is appropriate for businesses to march in the parade and over the commercialization of Pride increased. Conversations are still being had over the role of companies and money in Pride today.

Days before Pride began, the Lesbian Avengers, led by Gunner Scott, held a gathering at the Parkman Bandstand on the Boston Common. There, led by Scott, was a group of fire swallowers. Scott, well-known in Boston circles, was the Executive Director of the Massachusetts Transgender Political Coalition, where he led a five-year legislative campaign to get the Transgender Equal Rights Bill passed, which did in 2011. The Lesbian Avengers would, in the coming years, hold the Boston Dyke March starting in 1995, which was designed to be an alternative to the corporatization of Pride. The Dyke March continues today.

***

As the 1994 St. Patrick's Day Parade battle began heating up again, the Massachusetts State Supreme Court ruled that gay groups could again march in the parade. The Veterans Council felt that they had no choice but to cancel the St. Patrick's Day Parade in response to the latest ruling by the courts but would wait until their latest appeal went through. This was the seventh consecutive order that the gay Irish group had won against the Veteran's Council. John Hurley, President of the Veteran's Council, stated,

> They will never, ever march down the streets of South
> Boston as a group again.

David O'Connor, who was a member of the gay Irish group, was disappointed in the decision to cancel the event.

> We think it would be a lose situation all around for the
> Irish-American people if there is no parade.

Chester Darling, the veterans' attorney, asked for a stay of the order until after March 20. He stated that if the Council loses the latest appeal, the parade will not happen.

> That's it, it's called off. That is not a bluff. It's going
> to be a big disappointment. It's sad.

The cancellation left civic leaders in South Boston and gay rights advocates disappointed that another organization failed to take over the parade and were equally mad at Mayor Thomas Menino for his failure to organize an alternative parade. In December of 1993, Mayor Menino said he would

> do anything I can to make sure the parade takes place.

However, he stated after an 11-hour attempt to get the parade to happen, that

> People advised me that because there was legal ac-
> tion going on I couldn't really get involved. I'm not a
> lawyer but I listen to lawyers. We're dealing with un-
> reasonable people on both sides. I thought reasonable
> people would come together on the issue.

Catherine Finn of the Irish American Gay Lesbian and Bisexual Group blasted the Mayor, stating,

> The Mayor's claim that one week is insufficient is us-
> ing an inaccurate timeframe. The writing was on the
> wall in December.

There was an offer on the table that if the gay group allowed the parade to proceed that, the city of Boston would find a sponsor for a new parade with gay participation the following year. This was rejected by the group, with Finn stating

> It seems some people at City Hall believe that our capitulation would be advantageous to the Mayor, but we do not intend to capitulate.

Hurley commented on the parade that:

> It is not a sexual thing. We have disallowed other people from participating, including the Ku Klux Klan. This is a family-oriented parade and we are going to keep it that way.

The St. Patrick's Day Parade did not go on in 1994.

***

With a proposed budget of $58,210 for 1994's Pride celebrations, work began with co-chairs Jim Kratoville and Cathy Pfeiler. The committee discussed whether it was still appropriate to have Moving Violations start the parade. They felt that lesbian mothers would be more suitable because politicians are beginning to take a more active look at Boston Pride. This change did not happen.

For the second year in a row, a reviewing stand was set up to provide prizes and trophies for the best floats of the parade. It was set up on

Tremont Street before the Boston Center for the Arts and included politicians to help judge. This year also marked the 25th anniversary of Stonewall, and so they themed the celebration "A Global Celebration of Pride and Protest."

U.S. Representative Barney Frank commented on how far gay activism had come in the last 25 years, noting that the movement made

> astounding strides. Given the heavily encrusted prejudice that existed before, I think we have seen more progress than any civil rights movement in this country.

This year, they celebrated two political giants as Grand Marshals, David Scondras and Ann Maguire. David Scondras was the first openly gay Boston city councilor, and Ann Maguire was a political activist and Mayor Flynn's liaison to the LGBTQ+ community in Boston. Unfortunately, there was not much else regarding the politics as, for another year in a row, most of the programming was entertainment, such as a lesbian Pride party on the city hall plaza and a movie at the Hatch Shell on the Esplanade. Nancy Nangeroni, a transgender community activist and founder of GenderTalk Radio, which was an award-winning broadcast from 1995-2006 at WMBR, was one of only seven who spoke at the post-parade rally.

> Thank you, my friends everywhere, for inviting me to this party. Without you, I would still be cowering in shame. Someone once asked me, "Are you really queer?" And I said, "Honey, I'm a transsexual. If that isn't queer, I don't know what is." And they asked

me," Are you REALLY proud to be Transgendered?"
And I said, "Am I proud? You mean, am I proud to
be uncovering the truth about gender? Am I proud
to be exposing beliefs that are not true? Am I proud
to have made peace with myself, and to be sharing it
with others? Am I proud to be pursuing a life that
keeps me growing? Am I proud to have found the
courage to show my true nature? And am I proud to
be associated with others like myself? You're damned
right I'm proud." So to all those who still hide their
true beauty, To those who care about where our society is heading, And especially those who fear for
the welfare of their families, Hear us today and take
heart. Whatever your color, size, ability, beliefs, origin,
language, income, gender, sexual orientation, or your
special interest, join with us in cultivating Pride and
freedom of expression for everyone.

***

In January 1995, a U.S. District Court judge dealt a blow to the
LGBTQ+ Irish community by allowing the Veterans Council to exclude the community from participating in the St. Patrick's Day parade. The judge cited that the exclusion of gay groups as a part of a
protest could be construed as an exercise in free speech. This ruling
set up a showdown at the United States Supreme Court with oral
arguments beginning April 25. John Ward, the founder of GLAD and

the first gay person to argue in front of the Supreme Court, looked back on the situation.

> This case was not going to win. I did the best I could, and I think I did a good job, and it wasn't going to win. But it was a first.

The Veterans' Council held their protest march on March 19 without the LGBTQ+ community or the Veterans' group with AIDS. The LGBTQ+ community held a separate event opposite the march and waited on the Supreme Court fight.

***

There were a few firsts to the 1995 Pride events in Boston. The Boston Dyke March by the Lesbian Avengers held its first year. Formed in other cities in 1993, 1995 was the first year it was held in Boston. Designed as a counter-event to Pride, it started when lesbians felt that they were being excluded from a predominantly male Pride series of events and its growing lack of a political focus. Dyke March participant Sarah Shreeves commented,

> There's a different energy being all women and all dykes.

Cheryl Schwartz of Somerville agreed.

> Dykes have always been in the forefront of political movements. We're taking our power. We're having a dyke march because whenever we align ourselves with men, we become invisible.

The second new event included Youth Pride in Massachusetts, held a month before Pride events began. This was set up for LGBTQ+ youth to meet, participate, and advocate for a better future for themselves and all LGBTQ+ people. The third first was the Pride Lights event, which was lit in front of the Boston Center for the Arts.

The Pride Committee 1995 limited the number and type of political speakers again at the event to only one-half hour before the parade began. Jim Kratoville, this year's co-chair, commented,

> People say they want Pride to be fun. They don't want it to be political.

Co-chair Jennifer English echoed this.

> By making Pride a solidifying event, we coalition-build. Regardless of our personal politics, we're cementing what powers we have within our community.

Warren Blumenfeld, author and activist, disagreed.

> Where has the sense of urgency gone when people are literally dying in our community? We as a movement

don't see AIDS as a priority any longer, and that's a shame.

Last year's Pride Marshal David Scondras was also in agreement with Blumenfeld.

> Marching in Gay Pride is a political act. Having gay
> Pride is a political act. There's nobody in the world
> that could make Pride a non-political day if they tried.
> It would be as impossible as it would be to make the
> Democratic national convention apolitical.

With a budget of $80,000, Pride events were more prominent than ever. There was a block party outside of Club Fritz, a dance for women at City Hall, a youth event at the State House that the Justice Resource Institute sponsored, and an AIDS Action Committee party at Park Plaza's Castle. The 25th annual Pride Day Interfaith Service was also held at Arlington Street Church. The Grand Marshalls were Harry Collings of the Fenway Community Health Center and Kim Crawford Harvie, the Senior Minister of the Arlington Street Church. Collings would become the Executive Director and Secretary of the Boston Redevelopment Authority.

***

On June 19, the U.S. Supreme Court unanimously ruled in support of the Veterans' right to decide who can and cannot be in the St. Patrick's Day parade using the First Amendment as its basis. Justice David Souter wrote that:

It boils down to the choice of a speaker not to propound a particular point of view, and that choice is presumed to lie beyond the government's power to control. Our holding today rests not on any particular view about the council's message, but on the nation's commitment to protect freedom of speech.

David O'Connor, spokesman for the gay group, decried the decision.

Many minority groups have been discriminated against through the ages and the discrimination has been upheld by the courts. History will show this decision was wrong.

Mayor Menino was surprised by the decision but ultimately chose to respect it. LGBTQ+ groups would continue to petition to get into the St. Patrick's Day parade every year, and not until well after the turn of the millennium would a group of LGBTQ+ people march in the parade again. U.S. Representative Joseph Moakley didn't want these hard feelings on both sides to fester.

I don't think you should judge anybody by one vote or one decision. We should look at what we agree on, not what we disagree on.

***

The management of Boston Pride was becoming more troubled as the 1990s progressed, and their finances needed to be in better shape. Just after Pride in 1995, 11 members of the Pride sent a letter to the Board demanding the resignation of Chairman Jim Kratoville. In the letter, the members alleged that Kratoville had mishandled several thousands of dollars from an event that was held on the Esplanade. They also alleged that he did not award two vacation packages that Five Star Travel donated. They demanded a full audit of all Pride organization dollars. He was also accused of being prejudiced towards women and lesbians. Kratoville, who was involved for ten years, and Pride treasurer John Affuso resigned, citing "personal reasons." Gregg Fraker and Sabrina Taylor took over as co-chairs of Pride for the upcoming 1996 Pride season. A *Boston Phoenix* article shed light on the Pride funds and exposed the mishandling of the funds, embarrassing the organization further.

***

The thought was that having Sabrina and Gregg take over as co-chairs would make Pride 1996 run smoothly. Little did they know that 1996 would be among the most memorable and controversial Pride years ever. With the Dyke March in its second year in Boston, there was a growing fracture between those who wanted a message of protest and those who wanted a more entertaining and fun-filled event with families and corporate participation. The controversy over Pride funds was still fresh in everyone's minds and was the talk of Pride as events began.

The theme of 1996 was "Pride Without Borders," with planned boat cruises and a commitment ceremony at Copley Square. With the parade starting in Copley Square and ending at the festival on the Esplanade, the format was changed to have the Boston Police Department's mounted patrol unit begin the parade, followed by Boston Mayor Menino and then Moving Violations. For the second year in a row, the Dyke March started their march first but then would join the parade. The Lesbian Avengers had a little surprise for the parade, which would be among the most controversial moments ever in Boston Pride history.

As the parade began, an unknown man marched along the sidelines of the parade on stilts, flashing his genitalia to the crowd. This man was swiftly condemned for his actions, but the police could never identify him. As this happened, several Lesbian Avengers jumped into the parade next to a float. Holding up a mattress, two women got on top of the mattress and started to simulate sex acts while others marched alongside topless. Many members of the City of Boston, including Mayor Menino, the Boston Police Department, and the Pride committee, were outraged. The Pride committee immediately put out a statement condemning the acts of lewdness.

> As Pride is an inclusive family and community event, inappropriate and unlawful behavior will not be condoned.

Mayor Menino declared,

> I will not tolerate it.

City Council President James Kelly demanded to know why arrests were not made at the event, and Sabrina Taylor vowed to help the police track down the offenders. Kelly asked whether officers,

> observed said conduct, and if so, who determined that the law against nudity and open and lewd conduct...not been forced.

Robert O'Toole, a spokesman for the Boston Police Department, stated that he was unaware if the officers had seen the displays of sexual acts, and even if they had, the officers would have to make "judgment calls."

> What you've got is a nonviolent crime being committed in front of you. In situations such as that, there isn't a hard-and-fast 'lock 'em up' rule.

Gay activist Abner Mason remarked,

> I would hope most people would see this isolated incident for what it is; a throwback to an old way of thinking. It doesn't represent the behavior or thoughts of the vast majority of gay people, who believe that type of extreme, extreme behavior is unhelpful, dumb, and silly.

The Dyke March Committee stood behind the women who went topless and simulated sex acts. In a letter to the LGBTQ+ community, they stated

> In the spirit of visibility, we applaud, as should everyone, people who have the courage to express their sexual liberation through creative street theatre (the bed) or in any other form they choose. The dominant heterosexual world represses our rights to sexual expression daily. When Pride, Inc. does the same, they betray our lives and our passion. Pride, Inc. is attempting to gain power through assimilation.

Heather Janules, a member of the Lesbian Avengers who took part in what is now known as Bedgate, wrote a letter talking to those "who didn't get it."

> Pride, Inc. has apologized on television for the sexual nature of some contingents in Boston Pride, including The Bed. This disappoints me. The emphasis on gay marriage and the hyper visibility of straight-looking, straight-acting gays and lesbians in Boston Pride suggest that Beantown queers are emulating the straight world for acceptance. To truly exist "without borders," we must stop apologizing for those who share our umbrella in an attempt to please those in power. To create true unity, we must regard living "without borders" not only in terms of identity (gay, lesbian, transgendered, bisexual, etc.) but also

in expression of identity (doctors, lawyers, bankers, prostitutes, leathermen, country line dancers and club rats). As activist Sarah Schulma nobserves, the more radical the gay community becomes, the further left, the closer to democracy, the center shifts.

She ended the letter by avowing,

> I am not sorry for my pro-sex stance or for my public affirmation of The Bed. I made my bed, and I would lie in it again. Unlike some participants in the Dyke March, I joined Pride Inc.'s march to align with both the feminist/freak community (where I socialize, worship, fall in love, and organize politically) and the more conservative factions of Boston's gay community (where I work and financially support gay business). I ask that Pride, Inc. be brave enough to do the same.

Boston Pride's committee needed to be more brave to do the same. *Bay Windows* released an editorial frustrated with the Lesbian Avengers' act as having:

> Mayor Tom Menino's presence at the head of that march was an act of respect toward this community, and he deserved respect in return.

The *Boston Globe* met the co-chairs after Bedgate for a quick question and answer session. They asked about what they learned after Pride 1996, and Gregg Fraker responded,

> That's going to be an ongoing discussion. We need to find out where our community does stand and find out some guidelines. As long as there is homophobia in our society, we can always be pointed out for doing something wrong. There is an overreaction when we had 45 church groups, 13 colleges, more than 25 corporations represented, and two contingents are represented as our entire community.

Sabrina Taylor noted,

> There are so many issues this community has to deal with – same-gender marriage, adoptions – but displays like this take away from everything and really set us back.

Bedgate may be remembered for its debauchery, but it also began the conversation around whose community Pride represents. This conversation would continue throughout the summer of 1996 and into the next decade.

***

In 1997, the Pride committee moved to change Boston Pride's name again, this time to Boston Gay, Lesbian, Bisexual, Transgender, and Allies March. The committee felt the old name did not match the individuals and groups coming out for the parade and festivities. Sabrina Taylor again helmed the committee and took a keen interest in ensuring women were a significant part of Pride.

> I'm looking for the committee to be...a microcosm of the community, so we're giving the community what it wants. When I joined the committee two years ago, I was shocked to see the lack of women on the committee and shocked at the percentage of women to men on Pride Day; it's glaringly different.

Taylor felt frustrated by last year's incidents and wanted to ensure that Pride would run smoothly under her leadership.

> It was very frustrating because I wanted to protect 'pride' and what it stood for, but at the same time, we (the committee) had to remain neutral. There's nothing we're going to do to make sure it'll never happen again. I'm not trying to condemn or censor anyone.

Frustration boiled over at a community meeting a week and a half after Pride 1996, with many members shouting at Taylor and the committee. Taylor had to state that,

> The Pride committee has not apologized for anyone,
> and we will not be helping any type of institution find
> anyone.

This did not quell the voices. The voices about who was running Pride were getting louder, and with Sabrina in charge, the hope was that the committee would metamorphose in 1997. Taylor acknowledged at the meeting that the organization running Pride had been unwelcoming in the past but that it was, in fact, the past.

All of the focus from the media from this point up until Pride 1997 was on whether there would be more lewd conduct at Pride. Boston Police made it known that they would not tolerate any inappropriate behavior and that if any woman were to go topless, they would be arrested. There was no law in Massachusetts or Boston about topless women, so the threat was an empty one at best.

As Pride festivities began for "Stand Out, Stand Up, Stand Together," the Boston Police Department put out another statement. This time, though, it was about warning gay men that serial killer Andrew Cunanan may potentially be in Boston. Cunanan had murdered five people, including fashion designer Gianni Versace, between April and July 1997. He never did arrive in Boston and committed suicide in Miami, Florida, in July.

Estimates for Pride are between 100,000 and 200,000 participants, many of which came out to see if another stunt like Bedgate would happen. The parade was changed to the term "march" to make it more political, as the last several years have been more focused on entertainment. Pride was going smoothly; however, organizers made a mistake. They forgot to book American Sign Language (ASL) interpreters to the determent of deaf participants. This was another embarrassing oversight for the committee. Barbara Ayers, who had organized volunteer interpreters for the last few Pride years, stated that she was only contacted two days before Pride to get interpreters.

> You really need at least a month. Interpreters need to
> get a general idea of the time frame and what's going
> to be performed.

With no time, the committee needed interpreters but failed to secure any. Several deaf participants discussed the possibility of storming the stage and stopping the performances when it became clear that no interpreter would be available. The six deaf participants instead went backstage to demand to know why there were no interpreters. The event producer began to cry, stating that this had never happened before at an events he had participated in, and went out and publicly apologized on stage. She asked if anyone had ASL experience and could interpret, and three Pride participants saved the day. When attempting to reach for a comment by various news organizations, the Pride committee could not be reached.

***

The plan for 1998's "Retro Pride: Celebrate the Past; Create the Future" was for the week of celebration and advocacy to begin on June 1. This year, Sabrina Taylor and Eric Pliner were co-chairs. Due to significant rain in May and June, Pride was moved for the first time to July 11 and had fewer participants. With all of the controversies surrounding Pride throughout the decade, conversations among the community were being had on whether there needed to be Pride or whether the events had reached a standstill; for instance, there was opposition to a parade permit in Lawerence, Massachusetts, with several members of the city council voting in opposition. The parade continued with 150 marchers, but people wondered if the fight was worth it.

To make matters worse, *The Tab* investigated Boston Pride's finances and discovered that the organization was deeply in the red, with $30,000 in deficits incurred through years of mismanagement and miscalculations. Former Pride committee member Vincent McCarthy stated that Pride was being "run into the ground." It took several business leaders, including Harry Collings, to bail out the committee's debt. This was surprising as the Pride committee was making it known that Boston Pride was the second-largest Pride celebration on the East Coast, the fourth largest in the United States, and the fifth-largest Pride celebration in the world.

Amidst the challenges, Pride 1998 also celebrated the achievements and contributions of the LGBTQ+ community. Nancy Nangeroni, transgender activist Leslie Feinberg, and Abe Rybeck, founder of The Theater Offensive, were honored as Grand Marshals. Their presence and speeches at the celebration reminded them of the community's strength and resilience. Nangeroni declared,

> If we want to stand strong, unshakable in the face of all opposition, solid against all attempts to undermine us, vigorous in meeting any challenge, we would be smart to stand upon the broadest possible platform. We cannot knowingly allow the persecution of any person for any reason. Ours is not a lifeboat which is in danger of being swamped if we take on one more drowning soul. Rather, ours is the relentless march of a civilization which becomes stronger with each

>additional body. Our march will not be turned back
>by the forces of fear and ignorance. Our direction is
>towards the day when all people everywhere will enjoy
>the inalienable right, without fear of repercussion, to
>choose who to love, and how to express and present
>themselves in the world. This is not some new idea,
>some new freedom to be won. It is a fundamental
>right upon which this great country was founded.

Pride 1998 had a few new firsts added to its calendar of events. The first Miss Massachusetts Gay Latina Pageant was held to great fanfare. It would continue well into the 2000s with Somos Latinos, who would sponsor Latin@Pride. Unity Pride, designed to represent all people of color who are LGBTQ+, was held by Men of All Colors. This, too, was a top-rated event that would go on throughout the 2000s. Unity Pride would be replaced by Black Pride later in the 2000s.

***

After the events of 1998, it was clear that the Pride committee, which had been struggling for the last several years, needed a change. This committee was known to refrain from returning calls and was primarily inaccessible to the community, along with all of the financial and other issues that had arisen throughout the decade. The decision was made for a clean break from this organization. A new organization was formed, with severed financial ties to the old committee. Armed with its 501(c) 3 status, the new committee was known as the Boston Pride Committee, Inc., they started building out their board of directors with Linda DeMarco, owner of the Boston Pretzel Bakery,

Carol Frederick, owner of Coyote Impressions, and Richard Gordon, of Boston Event Specialists. DeMarco commented on the change.

> We are a new entity. We wanted a cleaner vehicle for people to lend support.

She remarked that the committee is

> Trying to make amends with some people.

Adam Tanner, Pride spokesperson, mentioned

> Since last year, we're trying to bring things out in the open more. We now have a lot more people who have a background in finance. And we're trying to get a lot more of the community involved.

Jim Patterson commented that,

> Refiling as a new nonprofit entity was largely a business move, although there are political reasons for the move as well. I think that this is the first time in six years that the committee is debt free.

As many organizations were owed money from previous Pride years, they wanted to mend fences with these groups even though there was no legal reason to do so. Linda had worked with Pride the year before as festival coordinator and joined the board as treasurer.

By May 1999, the committee had raised $13,700 with an additional $45,000 in pledges. Fundraisers at local bars and a silent auction at Club Café brought in $7,000. Tanner commented

> We are rebuilding bridges and starting from scratch. This is a different Pride committee.

Because of the small funds, the focus of 1999 was ensuring the festival and parade continued.

Police estimated that 150,000 people attended Pride in 1999. The motto of "A New Era" fits the new organization in charge of Boston Pride and the upcoming millennium. DeMarco and the committee had big plans for the future and wanted it to show.

> We've got a new millennium coming up, and we wanted a new era. We're focused on making Pride a year-round event. We need a broader awareness. We're very political, but our political-ness has been kind of quiet. People think of gays and lesbians only when something bad happens.

The committee quickly realized how hard it was to keep controversy out of Pride. With minutes to go before the start of the parade, with Candace Gingrich, the sister of U.S. Speaker of the House Newt Gingrich, and newscaster Randy Price as Grand Marshals, a quarrel erupted. A group of Lesbian Avengers attempted to enter the parade with a mattress being pushed on a pushcart with strategically placed stickers over their nipples. Wary of a repeat of 1996, the committee and Boston Police had banned mattresses from the parade. The Lesbian

Avengers were blocked from pushing the mattress throughout the parade. Alaina Gutwitch, a group leader of the Lesbian Avengers, remarked,

> We were trying to bring the bed back as a positive symbol, with nobody on it.

Adam Tanner commented,

> The way the committee tried to look at this is, it's everyone's parade, and it has to be what's best for everyone. I have no problem with topless women, but other people do. And it's against the law.

Pride asserted that the Lesbian Avengers did not acquire a permit to be in the parade. Ultimately, the Avengers took the mattress off the cart and marched with it over their heads instead.

Another controversy broke out at the same time as the mattress. The Pride committee wanted a group of lesbian mothers to front the parade, but Moving Violations wanted their traditional spot at the head. Moving Violations explained that there would be safety concerns if motorcycles were placed between other people at the parade. They made sure to let Pride know that if they were away from the head of the parade, they would stop the parade. Pride decided to agree with Moving Violations but was not happy with the last-minute change to the parade order, with one committee member stating,

> It's the Pride parade, not the Moving Violations parade.

The new committee found out that running Pride was not easy and that in order for Pride to run smoothly in the future, they would have to work with the community and create rules and regulations that everyone would have to abide by. Linda DeMarco didn't know it at the time. Still, she would continue to be on the Boston Pride board of directors for the next twenty years, shaping events and making decisions that the community and Pride organizers would judge from all over the world.

CHAPTER 4

PRIDE IN PROGRESS: 2000-2014

The turn into the 21st century set up a time of normalcy in the LGBTQ+ community in Boston, with gay marriage becoming legal in Massachusetts in 2004, Pride events topping over 500,000 people in 2008, and corporations taking a keen interest in the LGBTQ+ community by sponsoring Pride events throughout the United States. The New Boston Pride Committee, Inc. saw an opening to correct the wrongs of the 1990s, and in many ways, it did, but it also saw a host of issues develop that could not have been predicted.

***

The year 2000 marked Pride's 30th anniversary, and it needed to run smoothly. Wilfred Labiosi joined the new board of directors as president, with Linda DeMarco continuing on as its treasurer. Money flowed into the organization, with gross receipts at $129,197, a high for organizations running Boston Pride. There needed to be a significant push to show that Pride still mattered.

Ten thousand people participated in the parade. This was a large showing, considering many years of controversy at Boston Pride. Joan Jett performed at Boston Common to celebrate, and many of the parade participants left the parade route early to get good seats for the concert. Boston Pride honored actor Wilson Cruz as Grand Marshal and Massachusetts State Representative Jarrett Barrios was the other Marshal. Wilson came out to his parents when he was 19 years old and, at the time, was best known for his work in *My So-Called Life*. By 2017, he was starring in *Star Trek: Discovery*. An observer of Pride 2000 noted

> I think there is still a lot of activism, but it is not as loud anymore...There aren't a whole lot of people who are really angry anymore.

The Boston Dyke March was still seen as an alternative to Boston Pride in 2000, with more of a desire to be political rather than entertaining. The only note of protest against Pride was a small group of born-again Christians who warned the LGBTQ+ participants of an upcoming apocalypse. These signs and protesters were largely ignored, with many taking their information in jest. Max Gordon, a participant in the parade, stated

> I might get a good tan, but I doubt I'm going to hell today.

While not the most significant celebration in Pride's history, Pride went as smoothly as possible with the new committee in charge.

***

It was becoming more evident that putting on Pride events was getting expensive and that more money was needed for Boston's expected size and scope. Even though Boston Pride was a not-for-profit, individual contributions from community members were lacking. To adjust to the lack of donations, corporate sponsorship, and fees were increased to fill the gap. By the mid-2000s, these sponsors and fees represented 90-95% of Boston Pride funding. Insurance for a week of Pride activities in Boston was $10,000, and the average event cost was $120,000. Boston Pride wanted to continue to put on more events, even if many in the community were looking for just the festival and parade, but even just a festival and parade would cost significant amounts of money to operate.

Pride 2001 was set just a few short months before 9/11. The events during Pride were slower and tamer than in previous years, even though Pride's theme was "Mardi Gras." There was a lack of edginess in the festivities, and while some felt that something needed to be added, others were still enjoying the events. An expected 100,000 to 200,000 attended Pride, with events spanning the week.

Events included a Fresh Fruit Production of a comic variety show, a musical called "Could Be Worse," A dyke night at Midway Café, a movie night at the Cheri Theater, a gay night at Paradise Rock Club, a play called "Too Tall Blondes in Love," a boat cruise, Mr. and Mrs. Gay Pride pageant, a brunch, and a remarkable women's dance at Faneuil

Hall Marketplace. Linda DeMarco was unbelievably excited about the women's dance.

> I will be dancing where Ben Franklin and Sam Adams
> danced.

While smaller than in the last few years, these events provided stability for Boston Pride and gave the LGBTQ+ community confidence that Pride had stabilized.

***

Pride had a special meaning in 2002. The events of 9/11 were memorialized throughout the United States with new nonprofits, pledge drives, the music industry, and even U2 at the Superbowl. Pride events throughout the United States followed suit, including Boston Pride. The Gay Officers Action League of Boston (GOAL) invited their counterparts from the New York Chapter of GOAL to march with them in the parade, which caused much applause from the audience.

Whether or not 9/11 had any say as to the numbers, roughly 100,000 people attended Pride. Jeanine Galloway, a Pride participant, thought that,

> Maybe people were just more apt to participate as a
> result of 9/11 as part of a comfort process.

Not everyone knew what the theme of the year was. Meryl LaTronica, a member of the Stonewall Warriors, wrote,

> If you were to ask me what the new theme was, I
> couldn't tell you, but it seemed that those red, white
> and blue colors persistently popped up.

Others commented that it was just nice to see more acceptance from outside of the community than ever before. Heather Roster commented to the *Boston Globe*,

> Every year it gets easier. Acceptance is definitely going
> up. We're not going back.

8-year-old Carlos Rios told the *Boston Globe*,

> I say, leave my mom alone. I love her just the way she
> is. We have to be proud of what we are, and we're the
> ones who have to decide what to be proud of, not
> other people.

Not everyone was happy with Pride 2002. A Boston-based lesbian burlesque troupe named The Princesses of Porn wanted to perform at the festival on the common, only for the committee to decline. Amie Evans of The Princesses of Porn stated

> We need to not cut off part of our community to make
> it acceptable to the mainstream.

This was similar to comments made in the 1990s about what Pride should or should not represent to the masses. The Pride committee would continue to shape Pride into its image in the years to come by making decisions about who could and could not participate and in what ways.

Linda DeMarco took over as both President and Treasurer of Boston Pride and took a blended approach to raising the funds needed for Pride. Mark Taggert, who was in charge of Massachusetts Youth Pride, criticized Pride as commercialized and said that Youth Pride was the only event that did not focus on alcohol and money. Youth Pride was in its 8th year in 2002 and showed that there are other ways to have Pride events.

> Unlike a lot of adult prides-and I'm a huge fan of them-this is not brought to you by liquor and lube. We wanted to leave out the commercial aspect entirely and bring in entertainers and speakers relevant to youth.

Commercialization would remain in Pride events in Boston and increase significantly over the next decade. The Pride committee did try to accept donations but was unsuccessful in gathering the money needed to continue Pride. In their 2002 Pride Guide, they asked the public

> Help us stay visible and vigilant within our community by supporting the work we are doing. When you see the large rainbow flag being carried through the Parade route, please support our efforts by giving

a "buck for Pride." In addition, look for the Pride
committee donation buckets stationed at the Boston
Common.

While some donations were given, not much was garnered through
the committee's attempts to use the buckets to elicit donations.

***

In late 2002, the United States Supreme Court chose to hear arguments on sodomy laws, which was heard in March 2003. These laws
outlawed certain sexual acts, including acts by persons of the same
sex. Massachusetts was among the states that had laws on its books
that criminalized sodomy. This was both a welcomed and daunting
moment for the LGBTQ community. On the one hand, should these
be overturned, it would become a prelude to gay marriage.

On the other hand, a vote to uphold these laws would set the
community back. The Supreme Court's decision would come in June
2003, before Pride season. In Massachusetts, a challenge to the ban
on gay marriage was heard around the same time, with the hope that
marriage would be legal in Massachusetts.

2003's Marshals were Gay & Lesbian Advocates & Defenders
(GLAD), Gunner Scott, James Bonanno, and Nancy Norman. The
day began with rain, which was not unusual in Boston in late spring,
but it opened up to the sun by the time the parade began. Several
contingents of the parade protested the Iraq War that started a few
months earlier by the Bush Administration. Two parade participants
chose to reenact the famous 1969 bed-in that John Lennon and Yoko

Ono had presented to protest. One of the marchers, Julie Bell-Elkins, stated,

> We hope Massachusetts will recognize same-sex unions.

Gavi Wolfe, the public education director of GLAD, said,

> This day is half celebration of the community and all we've accomplished, and it is also time to gather gay allies and take stock of what's left to be done. It's critical to ensure the protection of all of our families.

Many religious organizations also supported Pride in 2003. Pastor Tiffany Steinwert of Cambridge Welcoming Ministries wanted religion for all.

> Once you get zapped by a Christian who says you are going to hell because of who you are, many turn away and don't go back to the church. By having one church that caters to the queer community, we create a safe space for people to come.

On June 26, 2003, the United States Supreme Court voted 6-3 that sodomy laws were unconstitutional. This was an exciting time for the LGBTQ+ community and was celebrated throughout Boston and beyond. Because of the landmark ruling, the Massachusetts Supreme Judicial Court, which was hearing challenges to gay marriage, held off on a ruling to consider the U.S. Supreme Court's decision and what that would mean in this case. This would not last long, though. In November 2003, the Massachusetts SJC ruled to allow two people of the same sex to marry. This was the first time in the United States that a state would allow gay marriage. Challenges would come, but in May 2004, the state would begin issuing marriage licenses to same-sex couples.

***

There were still gay marriage fights in 2004 in Massachusetts, mainly around an obscure 1913 law that prevented out-of-state same-sex couples from marrying in Massachusetts. Governor Mitt Romney was against the removal of the law and gay marriage in general, but the Massachusetts Senate voted it down anyway. Governor Romney was booed at a Suffolk University commencement for his opposition to gay marriage. It would take until 2006 for the 1913 law to be struck down.

The 2004 Pride celebrations were joyous. The New Boston Pride Committee, Inc. brought in over $200,000 for the first time and used much of it to celebrate same-sex marriage in Massachusetts. The seven couples that fought in court for the right to marry were asked and rode in a lavender Duck Boat throughout the parade to much applause from the audience and participants. Along with the couples, the Freedom to Marry Coalition and GLAD were Grand Marshals at the parade, having been a significant part of why same-sex marriage was now a right in Massachusetts. Aandre Davis, the operations director for the Pride events, stated,

Since the November court ruling, interest in this year's Pride has been almost over the top. I think the whole community has been energized. One of our barometers of interest is [event] registration. Last year, we had nine floats; this year, we have 36. People-even straight people, want to show their support for this issue.

He continued,

The gay community needs an issue to rally around. In the mid-'80s to the early '90s, you had the AIDS epidemic in which the community really came together. But then, by the mid-90s, people were starting to live longer [with HIV/AIDS], and I actually had people say to me, 'Why are we doing this Pride event? It's a waste of money and resources.

Herve Tennessee of Somerville, attended Youth Pride a month before Boston Pride and commented,

Everyone is just so happy about gay marriage. It's really about time. I never cared about gay marriage before because I never thought it would happen.

Tennessee would travel to New York next.

I'm going to propose [to his high school sweetheart].
I don't see why people have a problem with that. It's
not like we're hurting anyone.

***

Governor Romney, in 2005, backed a Massachusetts constitutional
amendment bid to ban same-sex marriage won a year earlier. This
initiative would be fought in the media throughout the year, and the
LGBTQ+ community knew that this may have only been a short-term
win. This fight energized last year's Pride, but there was a marked
decrease in the number of participants in this year's Pride. Whether
this was because of the continued fight withering on the community
or the oppressive heat, the difference was palpable. It was fitting that
the theme became "Pride in Progress...What's Your Fight?"

The Attorney General of Massachusetts, Thomas Reilly, skipped
out on the parade. At the same time, a supporter of gay marriage, he
would also allow a ballot initiative to go forward banning same-sex
marriage through a constitutional amendment. He was running for
Governor and stated that he had a prior commitment. His rival, Deval
Patrick, chose to march in the parade to much applause from the
audience. The churches that regularly marched as individual churches
banded together during the parade, with hundreds marching under
the Unitarian Universalists banner.

***

It was another year of rain for Boston Pride in 2006. Same-sex marriage was still being fought throughout public opinion, and the 1913 law was months away from being taken down by a Rhode Island couple. There was much homophobia to be still dismantled. At the Macy's department store in Boston, they posted a schedule of Pride events throughout June in a window facing the street. Some homophobic people did not take kindly to this posting and left messages on Pride's answering machine. Some of these messages were death threats and were unceremoniously turned over to Boston Police to investigate. Macy's chose to take down the events schedule. These homophobic responses did not damper the mood at Pride 2006. Boston Pride put out a forceful statement on Macy's schedule removal.

> In our efforts to promote diversity within our neigh-
> borhood communities, Macy's department store in
> Downtown Crossing Boston came forward to join us
> in this effort. They offered us a window display of our
> events during Pride Week which had our approval, as
> well as theirs. Unfortunately, Macy's altered this win-
> dow display in response to pressure from an anti-gay
> group. Macy's actions represent a weakness in resolve
> on its part. We at the Boston Pride Committee are
> saddened by Macy's unwillingness to standup for tol-
> erance, equality, and the dignity of America's LGBT
> population. Among the changes made to its display,
> Macy's removed references to both the Boston Pride
> Committee and the AIDS Action Committee. Macy's
> indicated that it was concerned that the original dis-
> play offended a few of its customers. We find this
> hard to believe. Both the Boston Pride Committee

and the AIDS Action Committee are nonprofit organizations committed to promoting cultural diversity and community welfare. The Boston Pride Committee is primarily responsible for Pride Week in Boston: an annual effort by the region's LGBT communities to celebrate their identities, express confidence in themselves, and to reach out to the wider population through understanding and awareness. The AIDS Action Committee is primarily involved in efforts to combat the spread of HIV/AIDS and help those already affected. How references to these two organizations can offend reasonable Americans of any political persuasion is hard to comprehend. We suspect that the pressure Macy's received on its original window display was the work of a few extremist persons. Their bigoted stance should not be construed to represent the opinions of the majority of Americans. We believe that Macy's erred in hastily capitulating to an ideology of intolerance. We respectfully urge Macy's to restore its display window to its original design before the start of Pride Week's flagship events this weekend.

Macy's did not relent, unfortunately.

***

The New Boston Pride Committee, Inc. board was finally beginning to grow. For the last few years, the board had Linda DeMarco as president and treasurer and one additional person, but in 2005 and 2006, it grew to three. They had a good working relationship and created many policies and procedures to make Pride a more organized and accessible series of events. The board's size differed from what their 2007 reinstated set of by-laws required, but overall, Pride continued at pace. The board started to exert power, which had been developing for years.

Drag performer Hedda Lettuce was asked to perform at the festival. Drag is a normal part of Pride and LGBTQ+ events. However, before Hedda was to perform, the Pride committee asked her to clean up her act as more and more children were attending the 100,000-plus Pride events. Hedda berated the Pride committee for the suggestion.

The Pride Committee can eat my pickled ass!

***

In September, the Pride board started sending out a monthly newsletter. These newsletters kept people up to date with other LGBTQ+ events throughout Boston, ways to get involved, and updates on the wants and needs of Pride. They were always looking for volunteers, and this was just one of several ways to get people involved. They also had a fall open house, which was publicized in their newsletters.

In early 2007, a significant moment in Boston history unfolded when 62 state legislators voted to advance a proposed constitutional amendment to ban same-sex marriage. This sparked a fierce battle between the legislators and the newly elected Governor, Deval Patrick. His unwavering support for the LGBTQ+ community was a beacon of hope, as he became the first sitting Governor of Massachusetts to march in the Pride parade in 2007, a tradition he had upheld for the previous two years as a candidate. His stance was a stark contrast to the last administration, led by Governor Romney, who actively opposed same-sex marriage. Patrick, a night before the parade, attended an event for MassEquality and stated of gay marriage,

> Even if you don't agree with us about the rightness of the question, smart political people have got to appreciate ... if we don't put this question to rest at the con-con [constitutional convention], this is all we will do for the next two years. And there is an awful lot of other business, important to you and everyone else here in the commonwealth about strengthening this economy and our public schools and our healthcare system that demands the attention of the folks on Beacon Hill.

Governor Patrick was cheered on as he walked a newly formed route that took the parade past the State House. While people loved having Patrick in the parade, they were less excited about the route. Abe Rybeck commented,

> My dress is riding up, but you know, I am a fat old queen. That's what happens.

During the parade, a decisive moment of solidarity unfolded when the Daughters of Eris, a group of women who marched topless, joined the parade without a permit. Unlike during Bedgate, this defiance was met with resounding cheers and support. Many were eager to be photographed alongside these women, a testament to the inclusive and supportive nature of the community.

There was significant controversy at the Boston Dyke March that required the committee of the Dyke March to apologize. Performer Bitch was hired to perform at the march. Less than twenty-four hours before she was to perform, the performance was canceled by the Dyke Committee after they were told that there was going to be a planned boycott of the march. Bitch attended the Michigan Womyn's Music Festival, known as Michfest. This festival was known to be anti-trans and was protested for years. To quell some of the backlash, Bitch gave a wishy-washy statement on the issue, with the committee thinking that this would solve the problem. However, after consultations with the entire committee, they canceled the performance.

The committee read a statement about the incident from the stage.

> The Boston Dyke March has always been and continues to be committed to being proactively trans-inclusive. The Boston Dyke March welcomes trans women and trans men to join the organizing committee, attend all Dyke March events, and participate in the Dyke March. The Dyke March is for everyone! Our top priority is to provide a dynamic and welcoming space for participants of all sexualities, genders, races, ages, ethnicities, sizes, economic backgrounds, and physical abilities. We strive to create a place where political and social change can be expressed and inspired. The Boston Dyke March is a venue for independent queer artists, performers, and speakers, and we celebrate the diversity of views that is our com

munity. Not all the views expressed by the people on our stage are necessarily shared by the Boston Dyke March Committee. We want to acknowledge that some members of our community were hurt by our choice of performers this year. It was never our intention to make any member of our community feel uncomfortable, oppressed, or that the Dyke March is not for you. The Boston Dyke March Committee encourages on-going community dialogue about trans-inclusion. The Boston Dyke March is for everyone!

The Dyke March put out an additional statement on the matter on their website after the march.

The Boston Dyke March Committee would like to address ongoing public discussion regarding its decision to cancel Bitch's performance at the Dyke March rally this year. In the week preceding the Dyke March, members of the Boston queer, genderqueer, and transgender community began contacting the Dyke March Committee, expressing dissatisfaction about the selection of Bitch as a featured performer. As the week continued, many community members and organizations contacted the Dyke March, urging the committee to cancel the performance. By the end of the week, it was obvious that the unhappiness had become widespread and threatened to disrupt the spirit of unity and inclusivity that the Boston

Dyke March has enjoyed for so many years. The widespread dissatisfaction included many longtime Dyke March supporters, past committee members, community sponsors, and liaison groups. The mission of the Boston Dyke March is to provide a dynamic and welcoming space for participants of all sexualities, gender expressions, races, ages, ethnicities, sizes, economic backgrounds, and physical abilities. Because our mission is one of inclusivity and unity, we are committed to listening and responding to the voices of our LGBTQ community members. This decision made by the Dyke March Committee was in response to the hurt and sorrow expressed by a large segment of our community, and is in no way a statement about Bitch as a performer or dyke activist. Much of the public discussion regarding the Boston Dyke March's decision to cancel Bitch has come from people outside our community. The Boston queer and dyke community is committed to progressive politics of trans-inclusion, so feedback from the Boston community has been overwhelmingly positive. We are excited to announce that the 2007 Dyke March was the largest Dyke March in Boston history. The Boston Dyke March has been and continues to be for everyone.

***

Between 2007 and 2008, it was becoming clear that the Pride board was not able to maintain their by-laws, and they were abundantly aware of this. The adopted, restated set they produced in 2007 called for a board of at least five and at most nine members. They had at most four members serving at any time on the board. They were also kept from holding multiple offices for the president and the clerk. As the board president, Linda DeMarco also held the role of treasurer in the organization, which was against the rules of their by-laws. There was a by-law stating that you could have a position for up to six years, and it was getting to the point where no one wanted to take on some of the significant roles on the board.

The decision was made to safeguard the number of people on the board and re-write the by-laws to ensure the organization complied with them. First, they increased the board from four to seven by 2008. The second was a complete overhaul of the by-laws. They wrote in their need and purposes section that the organization was there to

> Fill the need for educational resources which promote public education and awareness of the personal rights and liberties of the lesbian, gay, bisexual, and transgender community. To study the nature of the lesbian, gay, bisexual, and transgender community and its relation to its non-lesbian, gay, bisexual, and transgender counterparts. To foster lesbian, gay, bisexual, and transgender culture. To foster lesbian, gay, bisexual, and transgender cultural events.

Only one of those purposes is related to Pride events. The others focused on a broader way for the organization to be helpful and knowledgeable about the LGBTQ+ community, with the potential to expand beyond Pride event programming.

Decisions were made about the number of board members, which has changed to at least four and at most seven members at any time. There was no limit to how long one could serve on the board; the board officers would be chosen yearly with no change mechanism within the board. This was an unusual, though not illegal, choice as 72% of all nonprofit boards across the United States have term limits built into their by-laws. There was also a removal of the president and clerk to hold up to one position on the board at a time. These decisions allowed Linda DeMarco, provided that she wanted and the board voted, to keep her position as president and treasurer for as long as she wished to serve. She would not step down as treasurer until 2016 and move between president and vice president until the organization shut down in 2021.

***

The sunny skies of Pride 2008 saw an estimated 500,000 people participating, a significant turnout that few Pride organizations had achieved. When asked about this remarkable success, LindaDeMarco commented,

> I think the weather played a role with a lot of it, but for the most part, Boston has embraced the gay community.

Governor Deval Patrick's daughter, Katherine, marched alongside the Governor, her mother, and her sister. She had recently come out as a lesbian, and marching with her family showed a sign of unity in support of her and the LGBTQ+ community at large. *Bay Windows* reported that the streets "vibrated" with loud applause as they walked past spectators on the parade route. Financially, Pride did very well at close to $250,000 coming into the organization, the most that had come in from a single year. There was talk during this time about how to bring the organization to the next level of influence, which would take shape throughout 2009 and 2010.

***

In 2009, plans began to submit a bid to host InterPride's 30th anniversary conference. This conference made sense to host in Boston, as the first meetings began in the 1980s there. However, the planning process to get a bid ready was a lot of work, with many moving parts, and it needed to be submitted in 2010 for the 2012 conference. This was also an opportunity to show other Pride organizations how far Boston Pride had come from its previous iterations.

This bid for the city to host InterPride had letters of support from Governor Patrick, Mayor Menino, the Boston City Council, the Greater Boston Convention and Visitors Bureau, JetBlue, Zip Car, and Hertz. The goal was to have the Sheraton Boston Hotel as its venue with an estimated expense of $98,850 to cover venue costs, speakers, administration and technology, publicity and publications, and staff and delegate supplies. They continued compiling information on the City of Boston and other required information throughout 2009 and 2010.

Pride in 2009 saw the loss of along time community member, Woody Woodward. Woodward died of ovarian cancer at age 64, only hours before Pride was to begin. Woody was part of Moving Violations, the motorcycle group leading the Pride parades, riding on a motorcycle with her rainbow-colored mohawk. Mayor Menino declared June 7 as Woody Woodward Day. He stated,

> She was more than just a champion for equality. She knew how to inspire others to get involved.

Daryll Drew, a member of Moving Violations, remembered her,

> It's only fitting that she would die on Pride Day; she loved this day. She called it the high holiday for gay people.

In 2009, the theme took a trans-centric approach. Called "Trans-forming Our Community," the community rallied around the need to stand up and solidify their support of the trans community. GLAD board member Joanne Herman forcefully pushed back on legislative losses for the trans community.

> In each of the states where marriage happened in New England, there's a trans bill languishing.

Keri Aulita, the New Boston Pride Committee, Inc. vice president, echoed these words.

>It's about time we stand up and stand with our trans
>families, our transgendered allies and friends and col-
>leagues and co-workers and neighbors.

It was fitting that the inaugural King and Queen of Boston Pride pageant was held at the Estate nightclub in downtown Boston. The winners rode on a special float at the parade, solidifying the LGBTQ+ community's commitment to the trans community. Only a decade earlier, Rita Hester, a black trans woman, was murdered in Allston, and the community wanted to show some progress in tolerance, understanding, and acceptance of the trans community in Boston since her horrific murder.

***

2010 marked the 40th anniversary of the Pride movement, which was celebrated in Boston and elsewhere throughout the United States. Aptly called "Riots to Rights: Celebrating 40 Years of Progress," many people looked back on the progress made in Boston and beyond. Massachusetts was among the progressive states with laws and regulations protecting the LGBTQ+ community. There was still much to be done, but Pride 2010 celebrated Boston and Massachusetts's progression thus far.

There was a sense that the younger generation of LGBTQ+ people did not know of the movement's history. Still, society had allowed them to live in a way that previous generations could not. John Ward, the founder of GLAD, remarked,

They aren't weighed down by a lot of baggage. They seem like ingrates, but they're just living their lives.

Keri Aulita echoed John's remarks.

It's a double-edged sword. On one hand, you're happy to see them leading happy lives. On the other, you wish they had a better sense of history.

Libby Bouvier of the History Project said,

I want to say everything is great and positive, but that's not true. Everything's fine for certain people. If you're white and middle class, life is OK. Other groups, like transgender, are still anonymous. Race and class are factors. Still, it's certainly easier than it was in the '70s.

Pride 2010 had also become a battleground for politics in Massachusetts. On a rainy parade day, Governor Patrick marched with his daughter again this year but was followed by his upcoming Republican opponent, Charlie Baker. He marched the crowd with his gay brother Sandy and his gay running mate Senate minority leader Richard Tisei, shaking hands with the crowd as they walked along the parade route. Many were impressed, and many were not. David Siegal, a then 27-year-old voter from Mission Hill, stated,

I think a lot of it is political maneuvering. What would sway my vote is if a candidate didn't march today.

Indeed, marching in Pride became mainstream in Boston and other large cities throughout the United States. While not accepted everywhere, in Boston, LGBTQ+ people were becoming normalized. Don Gorton, one of the Marshals of 2010, noted,

> Look back at our past...change was not inevitable. Activism has been our pathway to change.

***

The crowds were there for another rainy Pride in 2011, filled with rainbow umbrellas. One of the participants stated to her friend while cheerfully walking down the street,

> Well, you need rain to make rainbows!

The New Boston Pride Committee, Inc. had its best year yet in 2011, bringing in $307,774, a new high for the organization. Controversy hit Pride 2011 early on when the Boston Archdiocese at St. Cecilia's canceled a "We Are All Welcome" themed mass during Pride week. Many LGBTQ+ Catholics were frustrated and angered by the news. Marianne Duddy-Burke, who was the executive director of DignityUSA, made a statement,

> What an abuse of authority. I wish I could be surprised, but I am appalled.

There was a push for more religious LGBTQ+ persons to speak up and participate in the fight against prejudice and discrimination, many coming from the parade participants themselves. Episcopal Bishop Gene Robinson remarked,

> I think it is really important for religious groups to show up because religion has been the reason for so much of our discrimination and prejudice.

Many people attended the parade with their children, wanting them to learn tolerance early. Linda Santana made sure to take her children along with her partner to the parade.

> I'm trying to teach them as early as possible that it's OK to have a woman love a woman. I'm starting to educate them from the beginning.

***

A lot was going on around Pride in 2012 that would have lasting effects on Boston Pride for the remainder of the tenure of the New Boston Pride Committee Inc. The Pride board was getting ready to host their counterparts from InterPride in Boston in April and October with a theme of "Pride Links Us Together." The board was excited to have InterPride choose Boston as their host city and be part of the larger conversation on Pride worldwide. In a blog post, the board stated,

> Boston was chosen as the host city to pay tribute to the organization's fantastic feat of promoting worldwide Pride for 30 years. Founded with the intent of being the international voice for the LGBT community, InterPride is a global network of Pride organizations. Its annual world conference provides a physical platform for LGBT communities of every background and location to come together. This is an incredible opportunity and an important honor for the city of Boston. Boston Pride could not be more excited to be organizing and sponsoring the conference and has sought to further show its support and Pride by making it the theme of this year's Pride Parade and Festival: Celebrating 30 Years of Worldwide Pride Movement.

While preparations were getting underway for InterPride in late February, in Sanford, Florida, George Zimmerman shot and killed black 17-year-old Trayvon Martin, claiming self-defense and Florida's "Stand Your Ground" law. It took until April for Zimmerman to be charged with second-degree murder. Martin's death sparked national conversations about race relations in the United States and Boston. There would not be a verdict in the case until after Boston Pride, but the conversations around Martin's death were constant during Pride. Boston Pride was silent about the Martin death and Zimmerman case, not putting out a statement on the matter, which frustrated many Pride participants, especially those of participants of color.

On May 31, the eve before Pride week began, a U.S. Court of Appeals for the First Circuit declared the federal Defense of Marriage Act unconstitutional. While this did not end the Defense of Marriage

Act at the moment, it was uplifting in a year of tragedy. Boston Pride put out a statement on what this meant for the LGBTQ+ community.

> On the day before Pride Week begins, we at Boston Pride are encouraged that the U.S. Court of Appeals for the First Circuit here in Boston declared the federal Defense of Marriage Act (DOMA) unconstitutional. DOMA, which became law in 1996, defines marriage as strictly between a man and a woman when it comes to federal laws and regulations. This means that benefits that come from the federal government, like Social Security benefits and the ability to file a federal income tax jointly, are restricted only to heterosexual marriages. It means that many married couples in Massachusetts are being denied the rights that our heterosexual family members and neighbors enjoy. The past few months have been remarkable for those of us who care deeply about marriage equality and ensuring that members of our community enjoy equal protections under the law. As we begin Pride Week, with a flag raising kick off to be held at City Hall Plaza tomorrow at noon, we know we have much to celebrate. But the DOMA ruling reminds us that members of our community across the country and around the world are still struggling everyday to have access to rights and benefits that others take for granted. We applaud the three judges who have made this courageous decision and we look forward to the day when all are able to love and marry freely and without fear.

As the parade began in June 2012, U.S. Senate candidate Elizabeth Warren was a welcomed sight to the parade and much fanfare. She was attempting to unseat Senator Scott Brown. The crowd was enamored with her, shouting, "Warren! Warren! Warren! Warren! Warren! Warren! Warren!" as she walked the parade route, something she has done every year since becoming a Senator. As part of over 15,000 marchers, other political marchers were Deval Patrick, Tom Menino, Barney Frank and his partner Jim Ready, and Joseph P. Kennedy, III. Pride brought in another record amount, this time $440,563, primarily through sponsorships and fees to participate.

On July 13, 2012, George Zimmerman was acquitted of the murder of Trayvon Martin. This sparked massive protests around the country. The following year, and for the first time, the hashtag #blacklivesmatter was used. This hashtag and acquittal would be defined as the start of the Black Lives Matter movement, with demonstrations occurring for the next ten years, and is still part of the conversation today. Boston Pride was conspicuously absent from other organizations' responses in the wake of the acquittal. All of their focus was on the InterPride conference in October. Caryl Dolinko, Co-President of InterPride, commented,

> Since this is the 30th anniversary of InterPride's conference, we are going to celebrate how far we have come and also work on building a strategy for our future. The Pride movement has grown significantly over the past 30 years, and we all know how to put on great events and parades. In our next phase, Pride will additionally focus on human rights issues that affect the LGBT community around the world.

With that, the conference was held on October 3 through 7, 2012.

***

2013 started great for the LGBTQ+ community. For the first time in a Presidential inaugural address, President Barack Obama endorsed equal rights for the community. He stated,

> Our journey is not complete until our gay brothers and sisters are treated like anyone else under the law, for if we are truly created equal, then surely the love we commit to one another must be equal as well.

These words spread across Boston, causing much applause from the community. Linda DeMarco exclaimed,

> I had a chill going through my body, I was just so proud! My phone started beeping like crazy. People were texting, posting to Facebook. It was one of those statements, that you just didn't really expect to hear in an inaugural address.

Lee Thornhill, director of prevention and screening for the AIDS Action Committee of Massachusetts, echoed these comments.

> It feels like a genuine step forward. He's the first president that I've really seen integrate key concepts of

public health, social justice and inclusion of all citizens.

President Obama would go on to not defend the Defense of Marriage Act that was signed originally in the 1990s to prevent same-sex marriage, and with a looming U.S. Supreme Court battle on same-sex marriage getting ready, marriage equality was more than likely to become the law of the land in the next few years.

***

On April 15, 2013, two brothers, Tamerlan and Dzhokhar Tsarnaev, placed two pressure cooker homemade bombs near the finish line of the Boston Marathon. Three people were killed, and 281 people were injured from the blasts. Boston watched in horror over the next four days as police and the FBI hunted the two suspects down, eventually killing Tamerlan and catching Dzhokhar in Watertown, Massachusetts. Knowing that the city was still recovering from these events, the planning for Boston Pride, which was only a month and a half after these events, would have to be changed to fit the mood and recovery.

Yellow and blue filled the streets of Pride, along with the more traditional rainbow colors. Yellow and blue were the colors of the Boston Marathon that year, and it was fitting to see everyone come together. Carlos Arredondo, who assisted the wounded on April 15, was at Pride, taking photos with both Massachusetts U.S. Senators and members of the audience.

The first active professional athlete joined the parade to come out as gay, Jason Collins, along with his former college roommate, U.S. Congressman Joe Kennedy. Boston Mayor Thomas Menino was missing from the parade route this year; they had recently announced that he would not seek re-election after being Mayor since 1993. Unfortunately, his legs no longer allowed him to march the route. Hundreds of people watching the parade held signs stating, "Thank You, Mayor Menino!" for his work over the decades and the recent handling of the Boston bombing. It was also fitting that the first Pride night at Fenway Park occurred in 2013.

***

In January 2014, change was beginning for the New Boston Pride Committee Inc. board. Linda DeMarco was pursuing opportunities with InterPride, the global Pride organization made up of Pride organizations. With this in mind, she chose to step down as board president, moving to vice president while Sylvain Bruni was elected president. Sylvain joined the board in 2010, and the board thought he would be the best fit to run the organization. Sylvain was also looking to become more involved with InterPride and expand Boston Pride with Linda to become the leading Pride organization in the United States. This became the first time since 2003 that Linda DeMarco was not president of Boston Pride. Linda chose to continue as treasurer and her new role as vice president.

In 2014, the Pride parade was scheduled on the same day as the Massachusetts Democratic Convention. This led to fewer marching politicians than in past years and news coverage about politicians being forced to choose between the convention and the parade. However, this did not dampen the mood of Pride, with a considerable number of people in attendance. Sylvain Bruni commented,

There are more families, more babies, more couples.
It's more diverse than it's ever been.

While Bruni and the board initially believed that our events were diverse, it became increasingly clear that there needed to be more representation, particularly among people of color. This was a challenge that the Pride board had not anticipated, and starting in 2015, it would prove to be a significant issue in the years to come.

CHAPTER 5

THE FALL OF THE RAINBOW: 2015-2021

A t the tail end of 2014, it was announced that the board would produce, publish, and distribute a yearly Boston Pride Guide to inform the public about events during Pride and other information about the LGBTQ+ community. While this is not the first time Boston Pride has had a guide, this is the first time the board and committee would solely produce it. Sylvian Bruni was particularly proud of this accomplishment.

> This is an incredibly exciting new venture for Boston Pride, which will allow us to deliver high-quality content and information to our community in Greater Boston and beyond. This is a Pride Guide by and for the community in all its diversity, so we invite anyone interested in submitting their ideas to contact us.

Linda DeMarco also commented on the news.

> The publication will be a full-color, glossy magazine that informs the community about Boston Pride Week, that raises awareness about other programs of Boston Pride, and that provides new and advanced content to many readership groups.

This new in-house guide had articles from community members, a complete list of events, and a lot of advertisement space. This was a prime opportunity to make more money for the increasing costs of putting on Pride and to expand Pride's programming. In 2015, of the 148 pages in the guide, nearly 30% of them were advertisements. By 2019, the guide had expanded to 172 pages, with over 45% of the pages being advertisements.

Questions were beginning to circulate about how commercialized Boston Pride had become. This was familiar to either Boston Pride or any of the larger Prides. Articles were coming out throughout the latter half of the 2010s critical of the push for more money in Pride and that Pride had lost its historical roots. Bruni had even pushed back on this in the 2019 Boston Pride Guide, stating that

> Individual giving (i.e., private donations from people to the organization) has rarely been successful for our organization. While Pride used to get over $5,000 of donations thrown onto the Parade's large rainbow flag, we now were lucky to get $10. Our orange bucket collections during the Parade and the Festival experience the same sobering lack of success year after year.

He argued that Boston had no choice but to put on the Pride it wanted using corporate sponsorship and fees, as no one else was willing to donate to the organization.

> Radical activists will tell you that you can always plan Pride without money. Certainly. But what kind of Pride? Without money, what do we cut from our 49-year-old celebration? The Concert, which attracts an average 50,000 per year? The block parties? The Black and Latinx Pride events, which typically lose money but provide essential space for the community? Would the community be amenable to forgoing a march completely as even one lacking the bells and whistles requires permits and security fees?

This Pride Guide concept financially succeeded the organization with $485,850 earned in 2015. Bruni was still working on expanding their financial footprint, and for Bruni's second act, he developed, along with the board, the first Boston Pride Gala. The gala was held at the Courtyard Boston Downtown Hotel on June 5, 2015. It was designed as a high-end event with politicians and LGBTQ+ elites and included a VIP cocktail hour and dinner. The gala honored two of Boston Pride's supporters, Mayor Thomas Menino and Harry Collings. This gala was expensive, with VIP tickets at $250 per person and dinner at $150 per person. These prices put much of the community out of attendance.

***

Two significant things happened throughout the first half of 2015 as Pride was finalized and put on. The first was the continued protests in support of Black lives around the United States. In March 2015, the United States Department of Justice released its full report on what had happened in Ferguson, Missouri, when 18-year-old Michael Brown was fatally shot by Darren Wilson of the Ferguson Police Department a year earlier. In April, Freddie Gray was killed while in police custody in Baltimore, Maryland. Black Lives Matter protesters were finding both opportune and inopportune times to stage protests, including in Boston. The second was that the Supreme Court was hearing in April and deciding in June on whether a ban on gay marriage was constitutional or not. These factors would affect Pride in 2015 and throughout the next several years.

On April 28, 2015, arguments were heard on same-sex marriage, and on June 26, 2015, the United States Supreme Court stated that same-sex marriage was constitutional. While Boston Pride had begun before the decision, many were waiting with bated breath. Marriage among same-sex persons had been legal in Massachusetts for over a decade, but many wanted to see their LGBTQ+ brothers and sisters have the same right to marry as they have.

BostonPride 2015 started like many other Prides before it. The parade had been set to go, and people were excited to get the parade going. As the parade began, Black Lives Matter Protestors interrupted the parade for approximately eleven minutes to present a list of demands to the New Boston Pride Committee, Inc. and Boston LGBTQ+ organizations throughout Boston. They stated:

> Today, we, as LGBTQ people of Color and allies,
> are interrupting the 2015 Boston Pride Parade. We
> are living in a rapidly changing country experiencing

unprecedented waves of protest and dissent. We've seen the rise of the Black Lives Matter movement in response to the systematic degradation of Black lives and the murder of Black people. We've seen trans visibility explode and Black trans women become the most prominent spokeswomen of the trans community. We've seen the movement for same-sex marriage become unstoppable as federal LGBTQ employment protections stall in Congress and abortion rights are continuously chipped away. We've seen the most vulnerable members of our community, trans women of color, murdered at alarming rates and burdened with discrimination, poverty, abuse and unemployment.. ..And yet Boston Pride remains the same.

We are a group of Black, Latin@, Asian, and white people, queer and trans allies who are interrupting this annual party to declare that all our struggles are interconnected. We won't wait for the advances of the most privileged of our community to trickle down to the rest of us. Trans women of color are being beaten down and slaughtered! In the United States alone, eleven trans women have been brutally murdered this year. Every two days, somewhere in the world, a trans woman of color will be murdered! Today, we act to disrupt Pride for eleven minutes to honor and bring awareness to the lives of each trans person murdered this year. We live in a society that has declared war on Black people, women, immigrants, trans people, poor people, and- at the intersection of all that - trans women of color. It is the duty of the entire LGBTQ community to stand united and prove that all of our lives matter.

YOU'VE GOT MARRIAGE - WHAT DO WE HAVE??

Our Demands of Boston Pride:

We demand fair and equitable Pride Fees.

It is an outrage that community organizations and nonprofits serving the most vulnerable of our LGBTQ community cannot afford to march. We demand a higher corporate rate that covers the expense and fees for small nonprofit organizations to participate in Pride. If corporations are going to use Pride to profit from our community, they can at least pay more for the opportunity.

We demand that Boston Pride take their hands off Black and Latino Pride.

We demand that the funding allocated to Black and Latino Pride events be free of interference from Boston Pride's predominately white board of directors, and used by the Black and Latino LGBTQ community as they see fit.

We demand more diversity in the board of directors for Boston Pride.

We demand that the board represent our community by recruiting people of color, trans people, and working-class people. We demand a Pride board as diverse as our community, and not solely comprised of wealthy white capitalist gays and lesbians.

We demand that corporate sponsors be approved not only based on how they treat their LGBTQ employees, but how they treat their customers and the communities in which they operate.

Big bank sponsors and participants are complicit with gentrification and predatory lending that have had devastating impacts on communities of color. There's no pride in corporate destruction of Black and Brown communities! We demand a review board of all corporate sponsors that will reject corporations that exploit the most vulnerable of our community.

We demand a Pride parade route that marches through a community of color.

Hosting Boston Pride in the South End and Downtown area purposely excludes communities of color and perpetuates the idea that communities of color are somehow more homophobic than white people. We all know better and demand a Pride that includes our neighborhoods!

We demand that Boston Pride remembers that Pride started as a riot led by trans and gender non-conforming people of color!

Our liberation as LGBTQ people isn't finished. Without the liberation of all oppressed people, it will never be complete. We demand that Pride themes focus on the political issues of our diverse community. We don't need more parties and meaningless themes. We need justice.

Our Demands of the Boston LGBTQ community:

We demand Boston's mainstream LGBTQ organizations hire more LGBTQ leaders of color in senior management positions. We demand more transgender women of color hired in leadership roles at Boston's mainstream LGBTQ organizations. We deserve shelter reform for LGBTQ youth of color and trans individuals of color. LGBTQ youth are overrepresented in homeless youth, and yet there is currently only one youth shelter in the area that accommodates their needs. We demand fully funded youth shelters and reform of the Department of Children & Families (DCF) to provide help to LGBTQ children from homophobic and transphobic families. We demand the mainstream LGBTQ community acknowledge the growing HIV and STI rates in neighborhoods of color in Boston. Despite the rates of HIV/STIs decreasing for white gay men, it has increased in Black and

Latino MSM and trans communities. We demand our community respond by developing an LGBTQ health center in a community of color. We demand accessible education and resources that aren't coupled with criminalization and racism. We demand all transgender health care, including gender-affirming surgeries, be included into MassHealth and all Massachusetts health care plans at no extra cost, under an informed consent model and without gatekeepers, especially for transgender minors. We demand our community come together to fight the recent closing of health centers operated by and for people of color, such as the Latin-American Health Institute (LHI) and Massachusetts for Asian and Pacific Islander Health (MAP for Health). We demand our community come out publicly against holding the 2024 Olympics in Boston. The Olympics will bring unprecedented gentrification, surveillance, cutting of social services, and punitive policing to our city. We demand more city funding be funneled to LGBTQ organizations of color and safe spaces. We demand our community finally acknowledge the systemic racism in this city. Boston is consistently listed by many media sources as one of the most racist cities in the U.S. We demand the City of Boston commit itself to ending the assault/harassment of LGBTQ people of color by the Boston Police Department.

The Pride board was pissed off at what just happened. Conversations among the board members, witnessed by committee members, saw them talking about *How dare this happen at Pride? How dare they interrupt the parade?* At no point did the organizers go up to or reach out to the protestors, nor did they listen to or acknowledge any of the protestors' demands. What they did do was complain to each other and the committee members that this had happened during their carefully orchestrated Pride event. Like many of the controversies of the past, Boston Pride chose to ignore it as there was always another year and another Pride to start prepping for, and the feeling was that the public had short attention spans for controversy in Pride. Articles were written in *Bay Windows* and *Windy City Times* about the protest and the broader conversation about policing. Still, there was no movement from the board on any substantive change in 2015.

In their blog post about Pride 2015, the New Boston Pride Committee, Inc. commented on its 45th anniversary, the 50+ celebration events, and the over 500,000 people who attended events. They also thanked the City of Boston, the various Marshals, including Erica Kay-Webster, David Bermudez, Samuel Brinton, Woody Glenn, Ellyn Ruthstrom, and the Boston Police. There was no mention of the protest, though the following was interpreted as a comment by the board on the protest.

> We want to thank our volunteers, our community partners, and our sponsors along with the City of Boston for making this our best Pride ever as they all helped us provide a safe and welcoming environment for everyone to enjoy and celebrate who they are.

It took until 2016's Pride before Sylvain commented on inclusion at Pride. He stated,

> Out of a board of five people, we do have two people
> of color on our board. We are trying very hard to
> recruit some more and to expand our board.

Eli Viva, interim director of the Hispanic Black Gay Coalition, commented,

> This year [2016], yes, Pride has started to add ad-
> ditional members of color to their organizing com-
> mittee and to their board. When I see those things
> happening, it's a work in progress.

This work would feel short-lived for Boston Pride as advocates would continue to push the board to make substantive changes, most of which went undone.

Samuel Brinton was an interesting choice for Marshal in Pride 2015. Brinton burst onto the LGBTQ+ scene in 2010 with a two-part interview and video on Brinton being forced into gay conversion therapy in Florida by his parents. By 2015, questions were beginning to be asked about whether Brinton's story was true or at least embellished. This was ignored by most of the LGBTQ+ community as Brinton started to work for organizations such as the Trevor Project, and while working for these organizations, Brinton would change the story. This was again brought up in 2022 when Brinton was arrested for stealing luggage at two airports while also working in nuclear proliferation for the Biden administration. Brinton received multiple plea deals and is out on parole as of July 2024.

***

In November 2015, it was announced that the board had created a way to give back to the LGBTQ+ community. Calling it the Boston Pride Community Fund, it would use the money from the block parties and provide grants from $500 to $2,000 to other LGBTQ+ causes and organizations throughout Boston and Massachusetts. This was initially designed in 2014 as part of the new initiatives that board president Sylvain Bruni and vice president Linda DeMarco wanted and were able to start in 2015.

As everyone got to work on 2016 Pride, controversy struck again in March and April with elected Marshal Anthony Imperioso. Put up for election by the board and committee, Imperioso was a member of the Woburn Police Department and president of the New England Gay Officer's Action League. He had posted on Facebook about Black Lives Matter protestors, stating,

> Maybe we patriotic Americans should start protesting welfare offices and blocking those entrances then these lazy illiterates will go away, Oh and by the way the police need to start locking all of those people up.

These messages were sent to Boston Pride through Twitter users, and Boston Pride immediately contacted Imperioso, disinviting him to be a Marshal for the parade.

When the committee discussed them with Mr. Imperioso, he indicated that he had made them. After a discussion between Mr. Imperioso and Boston Pride, his marshalship has been withdrawn.

The board wrote on their blog:

As an inclusive organization, Boston Pride does not condone any language that is intolerant of racial, ethnic, or religious differences. Additionally, we reject language that promotes violence towards any individuals who are exercising their First Amendment rights. It has come to our attention that Mr. Anthony Imperioso, who was elected a marshal by the community for the 2016 Pride Parade, has made some offensive comments on his Facebook page. Boston Pride cannot condone those comments. After a discussion between Mr. Imperioso and Boston Pride, his marshalship has been withdrawn, and Mr. Imperioso will not be a marshal in the 2016 parade. Boston Pride apologizes for the lack of vetting that occurred in the Marshal nomination process this year. Boston Pride is reviewing its marshal nomination process to ensure that it is both fair and robust to all members of the community going forward.

***

Pride 2016 was awash in happiness as same-sex marriage was now legal in the United States. Linda DeMarco commented,

The message is to celebrate the equality we now and to still strive in reaching equality not just here but around the country. And think about all our brothers and sisters in other states who are still fighting.

Massachusetts Attorney General reiterated these comments.

Pride is a reminder of the fight for civil rights. We've worked hard, and there's more work to be done.

Board President Sylvain Bruni noted the growth.

We haven't done anything different in terms of outreach and advertising this year than we have in the past. I think it's more of an indication of the growing attention that society in general is bringing to LGBT rights. As more and more people really want to show their support, I think people naturally want to support us more, and that's why it's growing.

Senator Elizabeth Warren celebrated her love of Boston Pride and noted that more must be done.

This is a day of celebration. I have my boa in the car; I am raring to march in the parade. But there are big fights to come. There is a man [Donald Trump] who hopes to be the leader of this great nation and he hopes to get there by hating others. The only way we beat bullies is we standup and fight back.

Many still felt that the corporate ties to Pride were undermining the original activist message of Pride. The Boston Dyke March has been trying to stay noncommercial, focusing on the people and issues at hand. Amber Clifton, a Dyke March organizer, stated,

> It's really important for us to stay non commercial, because we try to be very focused on the issues and people. I think that sometimes when you bring in a lot of the commercialization, the focus is a bit more split.

Major corporations such as Microsoft, Bud Light, Walmart, and T.D. Bank were now giving to Boston Pride and other Pride organizations nationwide. Fees to enter the parade were getting expensive, with nonprofits paying between $200 and $500 if they registered early. Last-minute fees would range in the thousands. The board would stick to its messaging that these fees and sponsorships were necessary.

There was also a significant sense of sadness in Boston and throughout the LGBTQ+ community at large two days after Boston Pride's parade as a gunman let out gunfire at the Pulse nightclub in Orlando, Florida, on June 12, 2016. Armed with an AR-15-styled gun around 2:00 a.m., 29-year-old Omar Mateen shot and killed 49 people and wounded 53 more. Orlando Police fatally shot Mateen after a nearly three-hour standoff. Boston Pride immediately put out a statement on the massacre.

> Boston Pride extends our sympathies to the victims and families of the tragic Orlando nightclub massacre and we stand in unison with the LGBT community of Orlando to condemn this vicious act. Today, at 4

> p.m.Boston Pride will hold a moment of silence at the Back Bay Block Party on St. James Avenue and at the Jamaica Plain Block Party on Perkins Street in memory of the victims. Boston Pride is working closely with Boston Police Department to ensure the safety and security of all the patrons of the block parties, which are annual events to celebrate Pride Week.

Boston Pride held a community vigil with Boston Mayor Marty Walsh on June 13 and had a benefit for the victims on June 20. Sylvain Bruni stated,

> The attack in Orlando reminds us that we must continue to be out, to be loud, and to be proud if we are to achieve full equality. We will continue to support each other and all of the members of our community by doing so.

***

2017 Pride was a mixture of sadness and joy. One year after the Pulse nightclub massacre, Boston chose to honor the victims with their own special float, where 29 of the survivors danced alongside. The float was adorned with 49 flags, one for each victim who was killed. The contingent held a 60-foot Pride flag. With a theme of "Stronger Together," Boston Pride wanted to be in solidarity with the LGBTQ+ community in celebrating life, mourning those who have passed, and maintaining a collective outrage over their deaths and any deaths within the community. Andrew Navaroli, a 20-year-old parade onlooker, stated,

> I think it's very powerful. I think it's cool that only a year later, They're able to claim their struggle and come out and show something good.

Sylvain Bruni told everyone that

> We are reminded every single day seeing what's happening around the world and around the country that any rights can be taken away and that there are still forces in our communities, in our country, in the world, that want to fight and put LGBT people back in the closet. That's why we are loud, we are proud, and we are very visible today.

These messages were almost overshadowed by a controversy of Boston Pride's making. A Boston Pride volunteer posted an interview with Juno Dawson on Attitude Magazine a few days before Pride on the group's Facebook page. During the interview, the transgender activist/author of young adult novels and non-fiction made provocative statements, including:

> I think there are a lot of gay men in the world who had the same personal misdiagnosis, because we didn't have the information that we have now. I think there are a lot of gay men out there who are gay men as a

consolation prize because they couldn't be women. That was certainly true of me.

The post frustrated many in the community, and they eventually removed the post after a call to boycott Pride events. In their statement, the Pride board commented,

> We acknowledge that our actions, past and recent, have caused harm to members of our community, particularly in the transgender community. We deeply apologize for using language and for posting content on social media that yielded such harm and pain. The impact of these actions has done members of our community wrong and caused divisiveness within our community. And for that, we are profoundly sorry. As an organization, we vow to be accountable for our mistakes and to our entire community: We will work to make amends, and to rebuild trust with trans members of our community; we pledge our commitment to ensuring that our actions do not perpetuate such harm or hostility. Boston Pride will continue to engage with individuals and organizations in the trans community to ensure that all our events are truly and fully inclusive, safe and welcoming of every member of our community.

This was the second embarrassment in two years for Boston Pride and another statement of apology.

***

After Pride 2017, the board announced through their blog that they would attend World Pride in Madrid, Spain, from June 26 through July 2. Bruni stated,

> Boston Pride's theme of stronger together continues to hold true at the international level, as we are truly a global community of LGBTQ people who are fighting for equal rights for all throughout the world. We are representing our great city of Boston where we hosted the largest Pride celebration in history and we are thrilled to be participating in the largest LGBTQ event in the world in Madrid.

While it was not a surprise that Boston Pride would want to attend such an event, it was a surprise how much they spent on travel and conference costs to attend World Pride. For a board of four, the price was a staggering $65,288, which exceeded eleven percent of their operating budget in 2017. There have been questions in recent years as to whether this could have been considered a work trip or personal, but for 2017, the board considered it a work trip. There were no noticeable benefits in future Boston Pride celebrations from what was learned from this trip to Spain.

After Spain, Boston Pride looked into becoming more global as an organization. Linda DeMarco applied and was elected InterPride's co-president in December 2017. Bruni was a regional director, elected in 2016, and having the president and vice president from Boston

Pride serving simultaneously pushed Boston Pride to the forefront of Prides worldwide. DeMarco said,

> It is truly an honor to lead InterPride as it has its roots in Boston where the commitment to advocating for the LGBTQ community is without question. I look forward to leading InterPride as we need to ensure that all Prides around the world are represented and have a voice.

***

The push for business as usual was palpable as 2018 Pride approached. In a lot of ways, it was. Politicians were attending more now than ever; the streets were ready, and yet another demonstration was about to disrupt Pride again. Under the name No Justice No Pride Boston, queer and trans people of color staged a sit-in in the middle of the parade. Their statement stated that

> We remind Boston Pride that Stonewall – led by trans women of color – was a protest against racism, anti-trans police brutality and the systemic oppression of queer and transpeople further marginalized by race, class, ability, gender, religion, and immigration status. As these injustices continue today, Boston Pride cannot ally itself with the institutions that inflict harm on our community. Pride should be an opportunity to uplift marginalized voices within the LGBTQ+ com-

munity and to work together towards intersectional justice and freedom.

They discussed the need to not take money from corporations that also give money to the Republican Party and candidates. Part of this was due to national pushes by President Donald Trump and the Republican Party to institute laws against the trans community and others in the LGBTQ+ community. The advocates also commented on the committee's use of police.

> Boston Pride has done little to address the police presence at Pride events, and the culture of Boston Pride continues to be one that centers the comfort of LGBTQ law enforcement while ignoring the QT-POC victims of police brutality and ongoing ICE violence.

Boston Pride had needed to address the cropped-up issues since 2015, and they finally knew it. The board was continually getting criticized, and their first step post-Pride was to elicit new members. Sylvain Bruni stepped down from the board, and the board added two new members, Steven Cullipher and Deborah Drew, in December 2018. Linda DeMarco took on the role of president of the board again. Unfortunately, this did not satisfy the groups asking for substantive change. Deborah Drew, in particular, frustrated the activists. Drew was a U.S. Army veteran and former secretary of the Massachusetts Log Cabin Republicans, which the activists felt was too connected to Republican politics and law enforcement to be on the board so soon after protesting police presence and the Republican Party at

Pride. The board only directly spoke in a press release announcing the new board members and ignored activists who brought it up. The board chose to employ a wait-and-see model for the controversy to see if it would blow over, something they have used for other disputes. Besides, the board had more extensive plans to take care of the 50th anniversary of Stonewall, which was fast approaching in 2019, and the events had to be perfect.

***

The 50th anniversary of Stonewall, a pivotal moment in LGBTQ+ history, required a large celebration. New York and San Francisco were getting ready to put on theirs, and Boston Pride wanted to put on a celebration as large as theirs. The board, through fees, sponsorships, and other means, was able to secure $874,412 to fund Pride 2019. This was the single most amount that Boston Pride had ever acquired for a year. Sponsorship opportunities included a $50,000 platinum package, a gold $37,500 opportunity, silver $30,000 level, Bronze $25,000 level, Black $20,000 level, with several more levels that bottomed out at the purple level of $250 just to be listed on the Boston Pride website.

Over 40 events were set up from May 15 through June 25 to commemorate Stonewall and all that was accomplished in the 50 years since those fateful nights of protesting and rioting against police brutality. The parade was massive, with 41 pages of groups participating from all parts of Boston and beyond. In all, 431 groups participated, the most of any year in Boston Pride history.

The parade went on without disruption, and the board felt a sigh of relief, thinking that they had gotten past the hurdles of the past. Things were looking up with a larger board, and DeMarco was back as president. There were still articles in the *Boston Globe* around the commercialization of Pride, but that was something they've navigated for years and could weather. What was not expected was a perfect storm of challenges in 2020 that would lead to the organization's downfall in 2021.

***

It was announced in late June 2019 that Super Happy Fun People had been approved for a "Straight Pride Parade" in Boston on August 31. With right-wing extremist Milo Yiannopoulos serving as their Grand Marshal, they were making the argument that heterosexuals were an oppressed minority. This did not sit well with the LGBTQ+ community. Boston Pride put out a statement condemning this event.

> It has become increasingly clear that the Straight Pride Parade is organized by a group of white supremacists and is an attempt to bait the Boston LGBTQ community, as well as racial and ethnic minority communities in Boston. It's a trolling event, designed to get a rise out of vulnerable communities. Boston Pride is not interested in responding to their bait. Our strength comes from directing our attention and energy to helping one another meet the challenges of intersecting oppressions. Boston Pride will continue to focus on supporting and empowering members of the LGBTQ community. We will continue to focus on the needs of people of color, trans individuals, and all those who have experienced racism, xenophobia,

> and sexism. We remain thankful for the estimated
> one million people, including our straight allies, who
> joined us at the 2019 Boston Pride parade and festival
> on June 8 and we're looking forward to planning our
> 50th anniversary celebrations for June 2020.

The event did go on, looking more like traffic than a parade. Protestors from both sides lined a few streets, but it was not replicated since its inaugural year.

***

2020 started like any other. The board was actively planning events, but by mid-March, it became apparent that this would be a unique year. The World Health Organization declared that COVID-19, a novel coronavirus discovered in late 2019, had spread to pandemic levels. President Donald Trump declared a national emergency within days, and industries were shut down. Not much was known about COVID at the time, just that it was killing people. Schools were shut down, public gatherings were canceled, and fear spread across the United States and the world. By early May, it was evident that Pride would have to be postponed.

On May 25, 2020, George Floyd, an African-American man from Missouri, was killed by police. Initially suspected of passing a counterfeit twenty dollar bill to a store was handcuffed with police officer Derek Chauvin kneeling on Floyd's neck and back for over nine minutes, not allowing Floyd to breathe. In the final minutes, he was unconscious and not breathing, with Chauvin not letting up or providing medical attention.

Protests broke out nationwide, including in Boston. The brutal nature of the arrest and death, mixed with the isolation and over 100,000 deaths during COVID-19, needed an immediate response. Black Lives Matter organizers planned dozens of protests, and organizations were lining up to support the change desperately needed when it came to policing, particularly policing people of color. By June 1, nearly half of all National Guard members were deployed for either COVID or protests. The Boston Pride communications committee wrote a statement in support of BlackLives Matter and presented it to the Boston Pride board for approval and to put it out. It stated,

> Boston Pride mourns the deaths of yet another recent list of black and brown people unjustly killed by police violence. The LGBTQ community is no stranger to the systemic racism, homophobia, transphobia, and sexism shown starkly through police violence throughout the decades. 2020 marks the 50th anniversary of Boston Pride. The first Pride event in Boston was held one year after the New York City Stonewall Riots, which erupted in June 1969 in response to persistent police harassment and violence. Fifty years later, the violence against black and brown people, especially black trans women, undeniably demonstrates ongoing structural systems of oppression and racism, reminding us that our work is far from done.

Racial violence in the U.S. is maintained, perpetuated, legitimized, and normalized by an entire system of entrenched social injustice. The 50th anniversary of Boston Pride calls us to honor the courageous, multiply oppressed LGBTQ people who risked their welfare to fight back. In its origins, the Gay Liberation Movement was a countercultural movement that understood all forms of oppression as linked. It is as important as ever for us to continue the hard work that is required to address the injustices all marginalized people face. In this moment is it especially critical to form broad coalitions committed to addressing the deep forms of structural racism that persistently manifest as forms of violence against black and brown people.

Boston Pride affirms its commitment to work toward a world that honors equality, equity, dignity, and respect for all people. We urge everyone to take concrete action toward dismantling institutionalized racism by vigilantly compelling elected officials to commit resources to anti- racist efforts; joining collective public actions that express the immediacy, importance, and magnitude of the problem; calling for the de-militarization of police forces; donating funds to anti-racist organizations; revising power structures within institutions; educating our friends, family, and community about how unconscious bias and institutionalized racism function; and persistently being the person in the room that calls attention to issues of social injustice.

Oppressions are interlocked, no one is free until we are all free. #blacklivesmatter

The board took the letter and chose to change what was written. Linda DeMarco explained,

[The letter was] a little too strong against the police, and we have a very good relationship with the Boston police.

While several parts remained the same, the hashtag #blacklivesmatter was removed, and the language was softened, including a line about the need for constructive actions. This reworked statement was made and put out by the board without input from the communications committee or consulting any person of color. The reworked statement read:

Boston Pride grieves the deaths of yet another list of black and brown people unjustly killed by brutal acts committed by people wearing police badges and uniforms. The LGBTQ+ community is no stranger to the systemic racism, homophobia, transphobia, and sexism shown starkly through inhuman acts of violence committed by some members of the law enforcement community throughout the decades. When we watch as a nation an unjust death of a human being we felt rage rising in our collective souls. 2020 marks the 50th anniversary of Boston Pride. The first Pride event in Boston was held one year after the New York City Stonewall Riots, which erupted in June 1969 in response to persistent harassment and violence perpetrated by members of the police. Fifty years later, the violence against black and brown people, especially black trans women, undeniably highlights the ongoing structural systems of oppression and racism, reminding us that the work is far from done.

Racial violence in the U.S. is maintained, perpetuated, legitimized, and normalized by an entire system of entrenched social injustice. The 50th anniversary of Boston Pride calls us to honor the courageous, multiple oppressed LGBTQ+ people who risked their welfare to fight back. In its origins, the Gay Liberation Movement was a countercultural movement that understood all forms of oppression as linked. It is as important as ever for us to continue the hard work that is required to address the injustices all marginalized people face. In this moment it is especially critical to form broad partnerships committed to addressing the deep forms of structural racism that persistently manifest as forms of violence against black and brown people.

Boston Pride affirms its commitment to work toward a world that honors equality, equity, dignity, and respect for all people. We know that in such a moment, words themselves are not enough. Words must be accompanied by constructive actions that elevate the voices of the oppressed and stand in opposition to those who use violence and brutality to suppress those voices. We urge everyone to take concrete action toward dismantling institutionalized racism in ways that could include:

• Joining collective public actions that express the importance and magnitude of the problem

• Give of ourselves to inclusive movements

• Participating in institutional reforms, including working within the institutions as an out community member, especially within law enforcement systems

- Educating our friends, families and neighbors about how unconscious bias and institutionalized injustice

- Being the person in the room that calls attention to issues of social injustice

No One Is Free Until We Are All Free.

We are #BostonPride #WickedProud

Athena Vaughn, a member of Boston Pride's Black and Latinx Pride committee, was appalled by the board's statement. Like the rest of the LGBTQ+ community, Vaughn found out when the statement was released.

> The first thing I thought was, 'have you lost your fucking mind!'

Casey Dooley, chair of Boston Pride's Black and Latinx Pride committee, was appalled by the decision and was even more surprised to learn that the hashtag #blacklivesmatter was on an earlier draft but removed by the board.

I've spent the last three years trying to rebuild relationships and apologizing for a lot of stuff I wasn't involved with. I feel like it all got ruined.

Jo Trigilio, a longtime volunteer of Boston Pride, commented,

We had put #blacklivesmatter on it. They took it off. I just felt like this moment in time is not the right time to be wishy-washy.

Dooley continued,

We wrote in that statement, 'We stand with Black Lives Matter. We stand against police brutality. The communications team then gave that letter to the board. The board then proceeded to take out Black Lives Matter and police brutality.

Judah Dorrington of the consulting firm Dorrington & Saunders agreed.

It was more than a mistake. It was erasure.

Trigilio unceasing,

The board members discussed it, removed it, approved the statement, and posted it. It was not an accident, mistake, or oversight. It was purposeful. Everyone should ask them why.

Henry Paquin, the entertainment chair for Boston Pride, agreed.

> Just when you feel like you have made some change for the better, the board makes another crazy statement that sets back the good work of the volunteers.

The backlash to the statement put out to the board was swift, both internally and externally. The board, within days, put out a statement that read,

> We hear our community and are committed to transforming Boston Pride to serve every facet of that community better.

The apology outlined three areas that were designed to assist in this effort. First, they were to hire the consulting firm Dorrington & Saunders to assess Boston Pride. Second, they would sit down with the Boston Police Department to discuss their presence at Pride events and to include not just Boston Pride board members but also members of color and the transgender community. The third was to sponsor the Transgender Emergency Fund. The board ended the statement by saying,

> We stand with the Black Lives Matter movement, and we are committed to dismantling systemic oppression

and structural racism. While these are the steps we have taken, more must, and will be done to transform Boston Pride into the organization our community is calling for. #blacklivesmatter.

***

The hope with the statement and the steps outlined was to soften the mounting frustration and tension. The statement was simply not enough for the volunteers working with the Pride board. Henry Paquin explains,

This is how Boston Pride handles community outcry on the tough issues of race and inclusion. They promise to do better. Time after time, these promises to do better are never fulfilled. Enough is enough. The current board doesn't have the capacity to address issues of racism.

JP Delgado Galamez, communications associate at The Network/La Red, observed,

Boston Pride is a reactionary organization. Pride didn't start showing they cared about Black people and People of Color until members of these communities, often also people who are queer and transgender, started doing actions like blocking the parade route. Boston Pride did not read the room when they decided to post a statement that didn't even meet the lowest bar of them all, saying #blacklivesnmatter.

Apologies from the Pride board continued to be put out across the media.

[We have] heard the voices of concern from members of the community regarding a previous statement posted on our website related to the recent atrocious events of the murders of Black and Brown people at the hands of police officers in so many places across this country. We deeply apologize for the hurt and pain we caused by our shortcomings. We pledge to hold ourselves accountable now and in the future. We acknowledge that we need to do more as a social justice organization to not only communicate our outrage, horror, and intolerance of these acts of police violence, but also to take substantive action to better address racism and white privilege within Boston Pride, the LGBTQ+ community and society at large.

Linda DeMarco reached out to the media to talk about what had happened.

All the existing board members have felt horrible about this whole thing that happened. But they didn't leave. Yeah, we are white. But we're not bad people. But we can do better.

Trigilio responded,

> I know that they feel like they've done a lot. But they didn't do the right thing. Boston Pride has a duty and responsibility to address the needs, concerns, and interests of its entire community. Boston Pride should be robustly inclusive. It has a long history of failure on this measure.

Paquin agreed.

> The lack of diversity throughout the Pride organization indicates the inability of Boston Pride to address issues of racism and white privilege. Until we have a more diverse board and an organizational structure that welcomes community input, the Black and Latinx communities will continue to be an afterthought of the board of Boston Pride.

Trigilio echoed Paquin's remarks.

> It takes only one or two meetings for a person of color to see that the Pride board does not center issues of racial justice, to experience or witness racist micro aggressions, and to see that there is no critical mass of people of color to enact change from within. Failing the Black and Latinx communities for so long is a clear failure of leadership.

Dooley noted that the board's response to communities of color was familiar in its planning and management of funds.

> Boston Black and Latinx Pride were underfunded when I began volunteering in 2016. When I became chair in 2017, I wanted to work in collaboration with established LGBTQ+ organizations of color. I wanted to work in partnership with them and support their events. But the board put so many obstacles in place. It was a constant struggle. There were no written policies for partnerships or for providing financial support to other organizations. And the rules keep changing. The process keeps changing. The board can say yes or no to any idea without needing to explain.

Trigilio continued,

> During 2017-18, Sasha Goodfriend and I went o n a listening tour, meeting with a number of LGBTQ+ community organizations and members who were unhappy with Pride, including BLM. We wrote a report that we presented to the Pride board. They responded by being defensive. Last year, I enlisted two colleagues to form a Pride communications team, hoping that we could begin educating the board from within. We had to battle the board to not remove words like 'oppression' and 'racism' from our external communications. We had to explain intersectionality to the board. Most recently, while everyone was post-

ing statements [about black lives matter and police brutality] all around us, we had to beg for days for permission to write a statement condemning police violence. After all these years of trying, my conclusion is that the board will not listen to change. My experience in working with the board is they experience community voices as antagonistic as opposed to thinking 'these are our people.' They treat that as some sort of attack as opposed to what it is – people asking them to serve their needs and interests.

Dooley noted that Black Pride celebrations were only given $5,000 per year, and most of that funding went to events in February, not June. She also remarked how Linda DeMarco would need clarification about exactly how Pride helped in other countries and continents. She stated that in a workshop, DeMarco commented that Boston Pride helped in "third-world countries like Africa." Dooley clapped back,

First of all, there are no third-world countries. [Third-world countries is a term no longer used to describe developing nations.] Second of all, Africa is a continent. The bottom line is that the board is not interested in centering the issues and concerns of Black and Latinx Pride. They are underfunded and neglected because they are not priorities for this board.

The committee members knew they had to do something fast, or the organization would suffer.

***

The committee members started to communicate with one another about what to do. The first thing they wanted was an explanation. Trigilio explains,

> The communications team and the volunteer work-force demanded an explanation from the current members of the Pride board. Instead of explaining, the board retreated to its bunker for two weeks.

DeMarco commented that

> It's a major volunteer organization that takes up an enormous amount of time and it's one of those positions where nobody is every happy with you.

Many of the committee members felt that hiring Dorrington & Saunders would not help the current situation. Dooley noted that the committee members gave other suggestions that they felt would make more sense.

> We suggested allowing the community to select a mediator to open a dialogue between the Pride board and the community leaders and Pride volunteers. You can't rebuild trust without talking to your workforce and the community you are supposed to serve. Instead, the Boston Pride board hired a consultant that

does not live in M.A. [Massachusetts] and is not part of our community. This is what you do when you want to preserve your power. It's another example of the board ignoring the voices of its own workforce and community members.

Trigilio confirmed her remarks.

Every time the community calls out Boston Pride for yet another racist, sexist, transphobic, or white-centered incident, the board says it will do better, then retreats to its bunker and waits for the firestorm to die. When the coast is clear, they resume their regularly scheduled program without making the necessary substantive changes. If this were not a publicity stunt, they would have immediately opened up lines of communication with their own volunteers, and with the LGBTQ+ community leaders of color who expressed unhappiness with their leadership.

The Pride board continued to hold firm on hiring Dorrington & Saunders, to the dismay of the committee members. The decision was made that something bold had to happen to achieve the change they sought. Athena Vaughn explained,

Evolution is inevitable. But it cannot evolve under the same leadership that's been there for over 20 years. It just can't.

Trigilio explained that the board has absolute power in this instance.

> The bylaws of Boston Pride give the board absolute and exclusive power. The volunteer workforce that does the work that makes Pride happen has no power whatsoever. The current board makes all the decisions by itself. It is not accountable to anyone – not its volunteer workforce, not its communications team, not the voices of community leaders and members. They have been practicing non-listening for years. Non-listening is a habit for this board. Habits developed from absolute power are hard to break.

Paquin concurs.

> It has become clear that [they] have no plan to ever change and it's time for the volunteers/committee members to stand up against a group of people not interested in listening to the community.

The committee members got to work on a new plan. This plan would request that the board resign from the organization. With every chair of each committee supporting the plan, they wrote and presented a letter to the board on June 16, 2020. This letter demanded that all six members resign and was followed by an outlined transition plan.

> By August 31, or otherwise defined by a Transition Committee, the Boston Pride Board of Directors

must transition to an entirely new board that includes full representation of Queer, Trans, Black, Indigenous, and People of Color.

· Transition Team: The transition from the current board to the new board will be guided and overseen by a Transition Team of three Committee members and three community members from QTBIPOC organizations of color. Members of the transition Team will be elected by the Committee. In addition to overseeing the process that guides the change in leadership, the Transition Team will also serve as the Nominating Committee who nominates six new board members.

Step One.

· Three board members, as directed by the Transition Team, step down by the end of June to make seats available to the new board members.

· The existing board elects the six board members nominated by the Nominating Committee.

· Pride board undergoes a transition period that includes training, mentoring, and orienting the new board members.

Step Two.

· The three remaining original board members step down after the transition period by August 31, or otherwise defined by the Transition Committee.

· The board and the Transition Team collaborate to nominate three new board members to create a board of 9 new people.

· The all new Board and the Committee undergo diversity, equity, belonging, and anti-racism trainings on a regular basis going forward.

· The first task of the new board will be to revise the bylaws (see below).

A Bylaw Committee be appointed by the newly elected board to revise the bylaws to create a more democratic governance structure. Revisions should accomplish the following:

· Share power with the Committee including veto-power with checks and balances.

· Establish transparent and democratic decision-making processes.

· Establish permanent seats on the board for the Chairs of Black Pride and Latinx Pride

· Include time limits for the total number of years served on the Board of Directors.

The board took very little time to decide, rejecting the plan put forth by the committee members. As a result, roughly 80% of the volunteer base quit working for Boston Pride, leaving many to wonder how Boston Pride would continue. Trigilio explains,

The statement asking the board to resign was signed by all of the chairs/leaders of the volunteer workforce, members of the communications team, and the LGBTQ+ community leaders of color. This means that the people who do the bulk of work for Pride no longer trust the board. And they are standing in solidarity with the QTPOC [queer and trans people of color] community who has been pressed for change for yours. Their refusal to resign is a perfect example of their inability to hear the voices of others. The community is speaking loudly, and they can't hear. They are busy trying to protect their power.

Dooley echoed Trigilio.

We explained how, if they would not resign, that we would be resigning ourselves. So over 80% of the volunteer force ended up resigning because the board came back and basically said...they won't be stepping down.

***

With their workforce diminished the Pride board got to work on hiring Dorrington & Saunders and reclaiming the exodus narrative. DeMarco began selling the consulting firm to the community.

The experience and commitment to the LGBTQ+ community that both La Verne Saunders and Judah Dorrington bring till help us fulfil the mission of Boston Pride to represent the full spectrum of the diverse community that we serve and to address structural racism and police violence in the region.

Dorrington also released a statement on working with the Pride board.

Dorrington & Saunders is committed to working with Boston Pride so that as an organization, they are better able to serve Boston's diverse LGBTQ+ community. We know that this work is challenging but necessary to promote equity, access and inclusion and enhance cultural competence, cultural responsiveness and cultural humility. Our focus will include issues of racial and gender social injustice.

DeMarco continued,

I am committed to making the mistakes of the past right and doing the hard work to make sure all our community voices are heard. The hurt I feel right now with what is happening with Boston Pride motivates me to make sure the transformation moves forward.

While the board was busy starting up a working relationship with the consulting firm, the volunteer base that had quit began figuring out how to keep the pressure on Boston Pride, for they knew all too well that the board would continue as usual. They developed a new organization called Boston Pride 4 the People, and the group was publicly announced in early July. It comprised 21 former committee chairs, co-chairs, and volunteers from Boston Pride. Announced by Jo Trigilio, they detailed,

> [Boston Pride 4 the People] is an organization found-
> ed by the volunteer workforce of Pride and communi-
> ty leaders who have lost trust in the current members
> of the Pride board to adequately serve the LGBTQ+
> community, especially the trans and LGBTQ+ com-
> munity of color. [We] want to preserve Pride, but re-
> focus back on the community, We want to address is-
> sues that affect our community – racism, white privi-
> lege, transphobia, etc. The purpose of Boston Pride 4
> the People is to bring Pride back to the people.

When asked about what Boston Pride 4 the People hopes to ac-complish, Henry Paquin stated,

> We are looking to improve Boston Pride by chang-
> ing the failed leadership of the board. We need board
> members who will listen to the voices of their own
> community and respond to their needs.

Trigilio highlighted what the board was doing while Boston Pride 4 the People was working for the better of Pride.

> Instead of starting an interactive dialogue with its own
> volunteer workforce and community members, the
> board hired a consultant from New Jersey to help
> protect their power. If they were serious about 'do-
> ing better' and 'transforming,' they would have done
> what they always fail to do, engage in dialogue with
> the community that is unhappy with them.

Between the exodus of volunteer staff at Boston Pride and the formation of Boston Pride 4 the People, another organization was formed
and put on its version of Pride events called Trans Resistance MA.
This organization was developed as a direct rebuke to Boston Pride
programming, highlighting the trans community and other groups
left behind in Boston Pride. Trans Resistance explains its founding on
its website.

> Trans Resistance was formed in June 2020 by a collec-
> tive of trans and queer activists in the Boston area who
> built upon years of contention with the Boston Pride
> board for being trans-exclusionary in their process,
> vision, and work and failing to equitably represent the
> magical TQBIPOC community in Boston.

***

While Boston Pride 4 the People began to organize, the Boston Pride
board wanted to clap back at the new organization and assert the
organization's dominance. On August 11, 2020, the Boston Pride

board sent a cease and desist letter to Henry Paquin, Casey Dooley, Jo Trigilio, and Valerie Bee, the organizers of Boston Pride 4 the People. In the letter, the board states,

> Several of your actions over the past month or so have been harmful to Boston Pride, and we must ask you to address and correct them immediately. Most importantly, it has come to our attention that you have been identifying yourselves as "Boston Pride 4 the People" in public forums and on social media platforms including Facebook and Instagram. As you know, the Boston Pride name has a fifty-year history; it is also a registered service mark. Your use of that name to identify your group, even with the added suffix of "for the people", is a direct infringement of our rights and may confuse members of the general public and members of the LGBTQ+ community who think that you are still part of this organization; our attorneys have advised us that continued use for that purpose could subject you to legal sanctions and financial penalties. Furthermore, we see that some former volunteers have been posting and appearing under the "Boston Black Pride" label and logo, which originated with us a number of years ago, is prominently displayed on our website and is creating the same kind of confusion.

In the letter, they stated that the board members rejected the call to have them resign from their positions and further asked the former

Pride volunteers to delete or destroy any Boston Pride materials, for their use could be construed as theft. Trigilio commented that,

> They are up to their old tricks. The majority of its own volunteer workforce no longer trusts their leadership. The community has had enough of white-centered, apolitical, corporate Pride. Pride belongs to the community, not the six people who are holding it hostage.

Boston Pride 4 The People complied with the cease and desist letter, removing 'Boston' from their name and website.

***

The Boston Pride board began its work with Dorrington and Saunders, hiring them in late June 2020, and spent six months developing a Diversity, Accessibility, Inclusion, and Equity Strategic Plan to help transform the organization. In December 2020, the board announced in a letter to the community that the transformation process had begun. They acknowledged their responsibility and that the board did not listen to the community, vowing to continue to expand and transform and apologizing for the past transgressions. They announced a few new positions that would assist in the process.

> You will see new opportunities for year-round community involvement in Boston Pride within the board, committees, volunteers, and advisors. We are immediately opening leadership opportunities including expanding our board roles to include a Di-

rector of Diversity, Access, Inclusion and Equity, Director of Human Resources, and Director of Technology. We are adding new Community Advisory Councils to guide and advise the organization, and are incorporating year-round diversity, access, inclusion, and equity training for Boston Pride and the community. In addition, we are evaluating and revising, where applicable, our bylaws, policies, and procedures. During this transformation process, transparency will be provided about these initiatives to our community through our website.

Pride 4 the People sent out a response to the letter stating that,

After six months of silence, the Boston Pride Board has released a transformation plan decorated with bells and whistles that attempts to divert attention away from the lack of structural transformation that is being proposed. This proposed 'transformation' process is merely a fancy performance designed to protect the absolute and exclusive power of the current board. It includes no structural change: no change to the bylaws, to the distribution of power within the organization, nor to the majority vote of the current board.

In response to Boston Pride's general announcement, Pride 4 the People instructed their supporters to boycott any new seats on the board and called for a boycott of 2021's Pride events. In February, The Network/L.A.Red announced that they would be boycotting, stating,

> After long discussion we have decided that until the Boston Pride Committee Board truly represents the diversity and beauty of Boston's queer community we will no longer participate in Boston Pride. We take vows to serve the whole community and to stand up to bigotry and intolerance wherever it appears. Institutional racism is EVERYONE'S burden to eradicate, not just those who are BIPoC.

Other organizations throughout Boston started to follow suit. A few, like GLBTQ Legal Advocates & Defenders (GLAD), held off until May to make a statement. GLAD stated that,

> GLBTQ Legal Advocates & Defenders (GLAD) joins in solidarity with Black trans leaders and former Boston Pride volunteers in calling for transformation at the Boston Pride organization. Pride is about protest, celebration, and community and should be a welcoming, safe space for all. Boston deserves a Pride in which Black and POC LGBTQ+ community members have a strong voice in leadership and which works to address the issues causing harm to our community, including systemic racism and police violence. Guided by our organizational values of justice and lived equality; inclusion, equity, and mutual respect; anti-racism; and collaboration GLAD will

not be participating in official Boston Pride events in 2021. In solidarity with Trans Resistance MA and Pride 4 the People GLAD supports the Trans Resistance March and Vigil for Black Trans Lives taking place on June 12.

DeMarco and the board started to reach out to community members to solicit help in any way possible to move forward. She reached out to Rev. Irene Monroe, a well-known Boston LGBTQ+ advocate, for assistance stating,

It would truly be an honor and privilege for us to have you help us in any way. I believe in the Pride movement. I have been volunteering in the movement for over 23 years. I am committed to making the mistakes of the past right and doing the hard work to make sure all out community voices are heard. The hurt I feel right now with what is happening with Boston Pride motivates me to make sure the transformation moves forward.

Monroe had received many awards in her professional life including the 2015 Top 25 LGBT Power Players of New England Award by Boston Spirit Magazine, the GLAD 2012 Spirit of Justice Award, and the 2013 Bayard Rustin Service Award, among several other distinctions so it was no wonder that DeMarco would want her to assist in any capacity she could. Monroe agreed to help the organization by recommending LGBTQ+ community members for potential board seat replacements and volunteering in other capacities. She believed that the board would eventually step down to make room for new voices, and she was surprised a few months later to find out that the change would not be as smooth as she would have liked.

DeMarco was adamant that change takes longer than people would want it to be.

> It takes time. It's an organization. We have fiduciary responsibilities. We need to keep the organization moving. We just can't all resign and not move forward.

Critics were keeping up the pressure on the board, accusing them of being white supremacists and going as far as reaching out to board members' employers to communicate their thoughts on how racist the board is. Surprisingly, the organizers of 2019's straight Pride parade offered to help protest later in the fall. The advocates turned down the offer of support. DeMarco commented,

> They wrote letters to our companies, [our] places of work, calling us racists. My family was taunted on social media and I was told they were going to cut my eyeballs. People who were not even part of the community joined in. The group that organized 'Straight Pride' wanted to join the parade and help with the protest.

***

With the coronavirus still raging across the United States and the world, the decision was made in February to cancel Boston Pride 2021. The regulations were still hampering the ability to gather, and it made sense to cancel with all the work that needed to be done to transform Boston Pride. Linda indicated,

> We had hoped to commemorate Boston Pride's 50th anniversary in June 2021 after having to cancel last year's parade and festival due to the pandemic. Over the last several months, we have pursued the difficult but necessary work of transformation and we want those efforts to be a central part of our Pride celebrations this year. Our community is concerned about racial equity, the resurgence of white supremacy, the needs of BIPOC members of the LGBTQ+ community, and the dangers that transgender individuals, particularly transgender women of color, face. We are inviting the community to participate in Pride with those concerns in mind.

With that in mind, the board started gathering people for the next transformation phase, a Transformation Advisory Committee (TAC), appointing seven non-boycotting community members on April 16. The application to join the committee stated the consultants would review them, along with the Pride board and staff, but were vague on the scope of their work, saying,

> The TAC will advise on the following areas:

· Diversity, Access, Inclusion and Equity

· Mission, Vision and Values of Boston Pride

· Intentions and Rationale of Boston Pride

TAC members will:

· Participate in the new Board recruitment process

· Attend events produced by Boston Pride to the best
of their abilities

The board allowed TAC and the consulting firm to continue their work while planning a June 2 mayoral forum for potential Boston candidates. The board made it clear to Dorrington & Saunders that there should be a plan for a power transfer, but they would not change their bylaws, leaving this to a new board. Dorrington was excited about the work they had completed thus far.

> We are not just transforming the board but the culture
> that will support equity for QTBIPOC people.

The Mayoral Forum that was planned by the board was being challenged by Pride 4 the People. After pressure, mayoral candidates Michelle Wu, Andrea Campbell, and Annissa Essaibi George dropped out of Boston Pride and chose an alternative forum. Two more candidates, Jon Santiago and John Barros, also attended an alternative forum. To limit the fallout from the forum, the Boston Pride board stated,

> We have been working since last year to take respon-
> sibility and change the systemic and structural racism
> affecting our organization. We have embarked on an
> inclusive and deliberative transformation process that
> is relying on members of the community who are not
> affiliated with Boston Pride to help us change.

After the Mayoral Forum's embarrassment, Linda DeMarco announced that she would be stepping down as President of Boston Pride. She did not mention when this would happen, only that it would happen sometime in the summer.

> [My exit plan] is a little accelerated now because I
> think the boycott is really hurting the community.
> Hopefully, the transformation advisory committee
> can get some members on board – and people who are
> boycotting us can step up to the plate.

***

After the announcement, TAC was getting frustrated with the committee and had concerns, including their ability to work collaboratively with the committee, their commitment to depart, a lack of transparency about their financial information, and their inability to reach a consensus on the issues. The board told TAC through Dorrington & Saunders that they wanted to take ten days to reflect but needed to be more specific to TAC about what would be happening during these ten days. Lee Santos Silva, one of the committee members on TAC, noted,

> We expected the board to address these concerns and answer our questions during their 10-day hiatus. Ten days later, I received a call from the board president thanking me for my work with TAC and informing me that the board had decided to dissolve Boston Pride. About an hour later, the news appeared on the Boston Pride website and other online sites.

AFTERWORD

BOSTON PRIDE FOR THE PEOPLE: 2022 - PRESENT

Boston Pride made a bombshell announcement on their website.

> For years, we have volunteered our time with Boston
> Pride because we care about and are passionate about
> the LGBTQIA+ community. We strived to foster an
> environment of diversity and unity within our orga-
> nization and the community. Over the past 50 years,
> Boston Pride has facilitated programs and events that
> have changed our society and promoted equality, but
> we know there is still work to be done. Over the past
> year, we have invested time and energy to address the
> concerns of the community, both with our Diversi-
> ty, Equity, Inclusion and Access work with Dorring-
> ton & Saunders and by forming the Transformation
> Advisory Committee comprised of members of the

LGBTQIA+ community to help bring change to our
organization. We are grateful for all who have been
involved in this process. It is clear to us that our community needs and wants change without the involvement of Boston Pride. We have heard the concerns of
the QTBIPOC community and others. We care too
much to stand in the way. Therefore, Boston Pride
is dissolving. There will be no further events or programming planned, and the board is taking steps to
close down the organization. We know many people
care about Pride in Boston, and we encourage them
to continue the work. By making the decision to close
down, we hope new leaders will emerge from the
community to lead the Pride movement in Boston.
This decision was made with a heavy heart, out of love
and hope for a better future.

Surprise, frustration, and confusion spread across the LGBT+
community in Boston after the announcement. Pride 4 the People
scolded the board for shutting the organization down. Henry Paquin
stated,

Today, we were disappointed to learn the board of
Boston Pride – who as of February, consisted of Linda
DeMarco, Martha Plaza, Malcolm Carey, Tina Rosado, and Deborah Drew – decided to dissolve rather
than work with us on a transition and respond to our
criticism with a real commitment to serve the community.

The executive director of MassEquality, Tanya Neslusan, mentioned,

> I had hoped to see a leadership transition rather than a dismantling of the organization. This will be a loss for our community at a time when solidarity is needed.

The Boston Dyke March released a statement condemning the shutdown, noting the funds given by the community.

> As one of the organizations working with Pride for the People, a group formed by former Boston Pride volunteers to reform Pride, we are appalled but sadly unsurprised by the statement released today by the Boston Pride board of directors. Despite being offered every opportunity to be part of the solution, they have chosen to disassemble Boston Pride. Instead of working with community leaders to change leadership without disruption to the organization, they have chosen to close up shop, taking, as they go, resources given to Pride by the community.

GLAD responded to the announcement with its press release, noting that

> It is disappointing to see the board make the choice to close down Boston Pride rather than work with BIPOC transgender community leaders, former Pride volunteers, and others to make room for new leader-

ship and needed transformation within the organization. We call on the Boston Pride board to be transparent in their plans for dissolving the organization and hope they will do so in a way that benefits the community and lays the groundwork for something new to flourish.There have long been calls from the community for needed changes in leadership and for Boston Pride to be more inclusive of Black, other POC, and transgender community members. Pride 4 the People, Trans Resistance MA, the Boston Dyke March, and others have been leading these calls and efforts for change over the past year and beyond, and we look to their direction for the next steps in this process now.

Dorrington & Saunders quickly pointed out that they had no idea that a shutdown was on the table and were under the impression that a new board would step in by late June or early July.

I didn't have anything to do with writing this announcement. This was the board. We and the TAC pushed them because they started dragging their feet again. We made it clear that until they were gone, nothing could move. June was the deadline for them to be gone.

TAC member Lee Santos Silva wanted clarification about what had happened.

> If the board couldn't commit to this level of work,
> I don't understand why they didn't just vacate their
> positions, leave Boston Pride intact, and let Dorring-
> ton and Saunders and TAC complete the transition.

The messages began pouring in on social media. Many were angry about the shutdown, some who were not up to date on what was happening over the last few years were confused, and many called the board racists and white supremacists. Several community members called the Massachusetts Attorney General's office to file a complaint about Boston Pride's funds. When reached out about complaints filed, the Assistant Attorney General responded with,

> We have identified a small volume of records concern-
> ing the New Boston Pride Committee that may be re-
> sponsive to your request. However, we are withhold-
> ing them in accordance with G.L. c. 4, § 7, cl. 26(f), in-
> sofar as they constitute materials related to a pending
> matter under review that reveal the nature and course
> of our review and divulge legal and other strategies
> and sources of information that, if disclosed, would
> cause a chilling effect on the cooperation of both the
> complainants and the entity. We note that because the
> exempt information is so interwoven within the text
> of these records, proper redaction would render them
> meaningless, and therefore, withholding them in their
> entirety is appropriate in this instance.

Most people were not sad to see the board leave. Kelsey Grunstra, the communications and fundraising manager of the Massachusetts Transgender Political Coalition, commented,

> We're not really sad to see Boston Pride go. But at the same time it does feel like a loss for our community to not have something happen and also to not have that 50-year-old infrastructure – this organization that has been doing this for such a long time – given over to people that deserve to be running that.

Hamel, an activist in Boston who goes by their last name, summed up the dissolution.

> It's important to take the long view. There have actually been a number of iterations of Boston Pride, and the dissolution of Boston Pride was just that really – the end of one era.

***

The former board was interested in talking to the media only in the statement released. It took months before DeMarco started communicating even small amounts of information. In November, DeMarco told Rev. Irene Monroe that,

> It has been a difficult few months with closing down
> Boston Pride office and all that goes along with closing
> down the organization. We did it for the betterment
> of our community and for the future of its leaders.
> While I appreciate your reaching out to me, I feel it
> is still too early to think about any type of story about
> what happened with Boston Pride and what is next,
> as that chapter has yet to be written.

Within months of the closing, Michelle Wu became the next mayor of Boston. She and others wanted some Pride celebration for Boston in 2022. A coalition of advocates and LGBTQ+ community organizations created a Pop-Up Pride celebration on June 12, 2022, on the Boston Common. This was a surprise to many but also a happiness that Pride could still happen without a single organization running it. Jason Wong, a participant in Pop-UpPride, said,

> I can't believe my eyes. There are a lot more people of
> color at this Pride than any I've attended since coming
> to Boston in 2012.

Other Pride celebrations began to "popup" throughout Massachusetts as well.

By 2023, many Pride 4 the People members began working on a new organization, taking back the name Boston Pride 4 the People under the tutelage of Adrianna Boulin as board president. Boulin, the Director of Racial Equity, Social Justice, and Community Engagement at Fenway Health was the perfect choice to lead the new organization as they started figuring out how to put on a Pride, considering that they would require large sums of money and an approach that is more inclusive of the LGBTQ+community. Questions about which corporations should be included were part of the early conversations around this new iteration of Pride. Trigilio notes,

> It can't be all in or all out; all corporations or no corporations; all police or no police. The middle ground should always be open for revision.

While not everyone was buying that argument, Pride went on in 2023 under the new guard. Boulin commented,

> We're making sure that everyone is at the table and we're walking humbly to always welcome other people to the table. We have a mission that specifically names educating people on experiences that Black, indigenous people, and all people of color experience. And we're ensuring that our history is commemorated. [Boston Pride 4 the People is] leading with inclusion and ensuring that we constantly have a growth and humble mindset. Boston Common has spaces more for youth and families, and our City Hall areas are more for adults. It's time for a unified Pride for everyone to enjoy.

Before Pride in 2023, the former board members Linda DeMarco, Malcolm Carey, Martha Plaza, Tina Rosado, and Deborah Drew sent out a release stating that the New Boston Pride Committee, Inc., which was to dissolve, would instead shift to preserve the history of Boston Pride. DeMarco stated,

> We want to make sure that the history of Boston Pride will remain on the record. In order to do that, we decided not to dissolve and continue to focus on that project. We are still in the process of developing our new mission, but our goal is to archive the history of Boston Pride and present it to the community.

It should be noted that the members chose to refrain from talking to the author about any assistance in writing this book or providing any data for it. DeMarco's committee also decided to only assist a little with the new Boston Pride 4 the People. Boulin commented,

> It would have been helpful to start with things like operational data and notes, permitting information, expense information, startup funding, etc.

DeMarco was still bitter about what had happened to her board. She and the former board,

> [Chose not to share any information] with a group that was attacking us and wanted nothing to do with us. Why on one hand did they want us to dissolve and go away, and then it was oh, wait a minute, we want everything you've done? The only people [from BP4TP] who have been approaching us are the people who led the charge to get rid of us. This is the group

>that got very hateful and nasty...they were the ones
>who caused the problem.

DeMarco noted that her organization provided the new guard with a 10-by-12-foot storage unit filled with materials.

In 2023, DeMarco was named to the U.S. Association of Prides Hall of Fame for her work and commitment to Boston Pride and the Pride movement everywhere.

***

Pride 2023 was a welcomed sight to see. Smaller than Pride events of the past, there was a festival on the Boston Common and City Hall Plaza, and the parade was back. While the Pride events were smaller, the number of people was large, with over 1,000,000 attending. While there was some controversy in 2023 and 2024's Pride with interruptions and protests over companies that provided funds to both Boston Pride 4 the People and the Israeli government and are against the ongoing conflict within Gaza, people were overwhelmingly happy about the events.

In a funny moment for Pride 2024, Jacques Bar had a parade malfunction and posted on X (formerly Twitter):

>We at Jacques would like to publicly apologize for
>leaving a f*ck*ng bus in the middle of the parade. We
>intended to ride it to the finish line, but it broke down
>and we evacuated like it was d*mn Titanic. We hope
>the city of Boston can forgive us in time, but in the

meantime, please come to our shows today at 3 pm, 7 pm, and 10 pm. Happy Pride.

It is still too early to see how long Boston Pride 4 the People will run Pride events, but it is in good hands. What will occur in the coming years will change the course of Boston Pride history, as it has every few years before it.

ACKNOWLEDGEMENTS

I wanted to send thanks to everyone who has participated in some capacity in the planning and execution of Boston Pride over its fifty plus year history, from the many volunteers to the Marshals, to the participants, and more. Without all of you, Boston Pride would not continue to be one of the strongest LGBTQ+ living monuments in the world. While it is impossible to thank every single person, the following are just some of the people and organizations who have made Boston Pride memorable:

Joe Abreu, John Affuso, Ron Allen, Susan Alves, Lianne Ames, Jim Anderson, Alexis Arquette, Keri Aulita, BAGLY, Thomas V. Barbera, Shari Barden, State Rep. Jarrett Barrios, Joseph Beckman, Jamie Berg, David V. Bermudez, Todd Bishop, Kevin Bolling, James Bonanno, Boston Sisters of Perpetual Indulgence, Adrianna Boulin, Chastity Bowick, Adam Brackman, Judith Bradford, Samuel Brinton, Sylvain Bruni, Michael Bryan, Stephen Burdick, Brendan Burke, Gordon Burns, Darryl Byrd, Peter Cann, Malcolm Carey, Linda Carford, Andy Cerier, Charlene Charles, Tom Chiodo, John Clese, Sharon Collinge, Bob Collins, Taffy Comer, Community Servings,

Alexa Cortez, Laverne Cox, David Crowley, Wilson Cruz, Steven Cullipher, Gary K. Daffin, Aandre Davis, Elsa Davis, Ellen B. Davis, Linda DeMarco, Maria DePalma, Dan DeSantis, Casey Dooley, Greg Doran, Deborah Drew, Cpl. Ciara Durkin, Pierce Durkin, Robert J. Ebersole, Drew Ellis, Joshua Ellis, Dan Emberly, Jennifer English, Melissa Etheridge, Beverly Fishman, Greg Frakir, Carol Frederick, Raffi Freedman-Gurspan, Linda Gallans, GLAD Legal Advocates & Defenders, Masha Gessen, Candace Gingrich, Ava Glasscott, Woody Glenn, Richard Gordon, Rev. Professor Peter J. Gomes, Don Gorton, John Graves, John Michael Gray, Keith Gregory, Tim Gregory, Ira Groelman, Cindy Hanslik, Matthew Hayes, Hedwig, Kristie Helms, Gavin Hilgemeir, Norman Hill, Rayna Hill, The History Project, Marsha H. Hotzman-Levine, Karl Houston, Joe Interrante, Lois Johnson, Marsha P. Johnson, Noel Johnson, Barbara Jordan, Leslie Jordan, Dana Kaplan, Erica Kay-Webster, Beth Kelly, Rev. Magorah Kennedy, Senator Ted Kennedy, Brian Kiel, David Knauf, Jim Kratoville, Ronnie Kroell, Janet Kyle, Stephen Kyle, Wilfred Labiosa, Marsha Levine, Gordon Linoff, Catherine Lohr, Ed MacLean, Craig Magaw, Michael Maggard, Ann Maguire, John Mahler, State Rep. Liz Malia, Jeanne Manford, Joe Martini, Massachusetts Transgender Political Coalition, Jeff Mattson, Howard Mayo, Vincent McCarthy, Ed McClain, Evan "EV" Malik McDonald, Tim McFeeley, Laura McMurry, Mayor Thomas M. Menino, Mark Merante, Steven Michalowski, Dale Mitchell, John Mitzel, Thomas Morganti, Jim Morgrage, "Fast Freddy" Murphy, Claire B. Naughton, Tanya V. Neslusan, Helene Newberg, Amy Nishman, Representative Elaine Noble, George Nolley, Nancy Norman, David O'Dowd, Dan Ortega, Pathways to Wellness, Governor Deval L. Patrick, Jim Patterson, Cathy Pfeiler, Eric Pilner, Daniel Pitcher, Martha Plaza, Kristen Porter, Randy Price, Katie Quinn, Ken Rickali, Michelle Riendeau, Bob Riordan, Charlotte Robinson, Melanie Robinson, Eric Rolfs, Robert Rook, Tina Rosado, Skip Rosenthal, Jefferey Roth, Richard Rubino, Bayard Rustin, Ellyn Ruthstrom, Cyndi Saint, Curtis Santos, Boston City Councilor David Scondras, Gunner Scott, Val Seabrook, Charley Shively, Sylvia Sidney, Craig Sorensen, SpeakOut Boston, Staci Stift, Lee Stone, Grace Sterling Stowell, Jeannie Sullivan, Thomas Surprise, Adam Tanner, Sabrina Taylor, Michael Thibert, Bernie Toale, Marco Torres, Kathy Travers, Diane Travis, Jo Triglio, Urvashi Vaid, Mark Walsh, Cynthia Walton, Sue Ward, Michael Wasserman, Carol Wessling, Edie Windsor, Nidhi Yadalam, Jacob Smith Yang, Richard York, Reina Ysaguirre-Boersma, Rob Zuromski.

Additionally, I'd like to thank the following people and organizations that helped in the research and writing of this book:

The Archives and Special Collections in Snell Library at Northeastern University, The Beinecke Rare Book and Manuscript Library at Yale University, The Boston Public Library, The History Project, Jo Triglio, Reina Ysaguirre-Boersma, John Mollica, and the University Archives and Special Collections in the Joseph P. Healey Library at the University of Massachusetts Boston.

Finally, I'd like to thank everyone who has kept me motivated over the years while researching and writing:

Timothy Bickel, John Gonzalez, Carol Fitzgerald, Nico Kurkjian, Katie Lindquist, Joanne Mastantuono, John Mollica, Juliette Ste Croix, Sarina Ste Croix, and my dogs Bella and Harry.

OH, and Netflix, Hulu, and Max for keeping me sane throughout this.

NOTES

(IN ALPHABETICAL ORDER BY CHAPTER)

INTRODUCTION NOTES

4 policemen hurt in 'village' raid: Melee near Sheridan Square follows action at bar. (June 29, 1969). *New York Times*.

Bouvier, L., & Krone, M. (2015). A history of Boston Pride. *Boston Pride Guide 2015 Supplement*, 1.

Ebbert, S. (June 30, 2020). Activists demand Pride board overhaul. *Boston Globe*.

Gay, Lesbian, Bisexual, and Transgender Historical Society. (n.d.). *Protests Independence Hall - Philadelphia, National- Homophile Organizations. July 1-4, 1965; n.d. TS Phyllis Lyon, Del Martin and the Daughters of Bilitis Box 20 Folder 32*.

GLBTQ Legal Advocates & Defenders (May 11, 2021). *GLAD Supports Trans Resistance MA and Pride 4 the People in Calls for Transformation at Boston Pride* https://www.glad.org/post/glad-supports-calls-for-transformation-at-boston-pride/

"Love Is All You Need, 1970," Documented. (1970). In: Digital Collections of The History Project.

The Network/La Red (February 2021). *Boycott Boston Pride: The Network/LA Red announces our boycott of Boston Pride* https://www.tnlr.org/en/boycott-boston-pride/

No room on the stage? (July 1997). *Sojourner.*

Phelps, R. (July 9, 2021). After 50 years, Boston Pride to dissolve, announces its board of directors. *Boston Spirit Magazine.*

Society of Professional Journalists. *SPJ Code of Ethics*. https://www. spj.org/ethicscode.asp

CHAPTER ONE NOTES

4 policemen hurt in 'village' raid (June 29,1969).

600 gay persons march in Boston observance. (June 23, 1974). *Boston Globe.*

Boston Globe. *Lois Johnson Obituary*. Retrieved September 20, 2024 from https://www.legacy.com/us/obituaries/bostonglobe/name /lois-johnson-obituary?id=6791182

Boston Police indicted for extorting gay bars. (February 1988). *Campaign.*

Bouvier, L., & Krone, M. (2015).

Bronski, M. *Shively, a Pivotal Figure in the Gay Liberation Movement*. Retrieved September 20, 2024 from https://lambdaliterary.org/2 017/11/remembering-charles-shively/

Bruce, K. M. (2016). *Pride Parades: How a Parade Changed the World*. New York University Press. Pg. 71

Bruce, K. M. (2016). Pg. 77

Bruce, K. M. (2016). Pg. 85

Bumblebee, M. (June 12, 1976). "Unity" theme of Boston Gay Pride Week. *Gay Community News.*

Campbell, A. (2019). *Queer X Design: 50 Years of Signs, Symbols, Banners, Logos, and Graphic Art of LGBTQ.* Black Dog & Leventhal Publishers. Hatchette Book Group, Inc. Pg. 74

Centers for Disease Control (1981). *Morbidity and Mortality Weekly Report*, Morbidity and Mortality Weekly Report, Volume 30 Issue 21.

Clendinen, D., & Nagourney, A. (1999). *Out for Good: The Struggle to Build a Gay Rights Movement in America*. Touchstone. Pg. 125

Clendinen, D., & Nagourney, A. (1999). Pg. 127

Cohen, A. The Boston/Boise Affair, 1977-78. (Essay). *The Gay & Lesbian Review Worldwide*.

Dignify Boston (1977). Gay Pride '77. MS 1779, John Mitzel Papers, Series 1: Correspondence and Research Files 1962-2013 Box 6 Folder 259. In. Beinecke Rare Book & Manuscript Library at Yale University.

Durham, M. (December 31, 1971). Homosexuals in Revolt: The year that one liberation movement turned militant. *Life*.

Eastern Regional Conference of Homophile Organization (March 16, 1970). *Resolved*. In: Digital Collections of The History Project.

Ebbert, S. (June 30, 2020).

Eisenberg, D. (June 11, 2011). 41 years of Pride: It really has gotten better. *The Boston Phoenix*.

Fenway Muggings. (July 12, 1973). *Gay Community News*.

Fosburgh, L. (June 29, 1970). Thousands of homosexuals hold a protest rally in Central Park. *New York Times*.

Gay Brother Murdered. (July 19, 1973). *Gay Community News*.

Gay Pride Week: Come Celebrate With Us. (1971). In: The History Project Archives.

Gay Pride Week '72. (1972). In: The History Project Archives.

Gays Respond. (July 26, 1973). *Gay Community News*.

Gay rights supporters hold march. (June 17, 1979). *Boston Globe*.

The General Court of the Commonwealth of Mass-achusetts. (n.d.) *Section 34: Crime against nature*. https://malegislature.gov/Laws/GeneralLaws/PartIV/TitleI/Chapter272/Section34

The General Court of the Commonwealth of Mass-achusetts. (n.d.) *Section 35: Unnatural and lascivious acts*. https://malegislature.gov/Laws/GeneralLaws/PartIV/TitleI/Chapter272/Section35

Goldfarb, S. (July 28, 2010). *Sam Goldfarb talks about his most memorable Boston Pride* [Interview].https://www.youtube.com/watch?v=yFnphpWvVDU

Hostile crowd dispersed near Sheridan Square. (July 3, 1969). *New York Times*.

Johnson, I. (December 7, 1974). Lavender rhino at last on subway! *Gay Community News*.

Johnson, L. (July 27, 2010). *Lois Johnson talks about early Pride marches* [Interview]. https://www.youtube.com/watch?v=dKK_zt1oa8Q

Kneeland, P. (June 27, 1971). March, speeches mark Gay Pride Week. *Boston Globe*.

Krone, M. (September/October 2012). John Mitzel Isn't Going Anywhere. *Boston Spirit Magazine*.

Kyper, J. (July 2, 1972). Gay PrideWeek—Towards a Community? *Boston After Dark*. https://historyproject.omeka.net/items/show/481

Lavender Rhino, I. (1990). The Official Guide to Lesbian & Gay PrideWeeks in Boston. In: Lavender Rhino, Inc.

Lopez, R. (2019). *The Hub of the Gay Universe: An LGBTQ History of Boston, Provincetown, and Beyond*. Shawmut Peninsula Press. Pg. 177

Lopez, R. (2019). Pg. 178

Lopez, R. (2019). Pg. 198

Lopez, R. (2019). Pg. 212

"Love Is All You Need, 1970," Documented. (1970).

Mason, A. (June 10, 2016). Are Pride Parade's Corporate Ties Undermining Its Original Queer Activist Message? *WBUR*.

Mitzel, J. (1970). Entry June 30, 1970. MS 1779, John Mitzel Papers, Series IV: Diaries 1961-2002 Box 31 Folder 830. In. Beinecke Rare Book & Manuscript Library at Yale University.

Mitzel, J. (1971a). Entry June 25, 1971. MS 1779, John Mitzel Papers, Series IV: Diaries 1961-2002 Box 31 Folder 832. In. Beinecke Rare Book & Manuscript Library at Yale University.

Mitzel, J. (1971b). The Lesson of Gay Pride Week: Beware the SWP. MS 1779, John Mitzel Papers, Series III: Professional Papers 1964-2013 Box 21 Folder 613. In. Beinecke Rare Book & Manuscript Library at Yale University.

Mitzel, J. (1972a). Entry May 7, 1972. MS 1779, John Mitzel Papers, Series IV: Diaries 1961-2002 Box 31 Folder 835. In. Beinecke Rare Book & Manuscript Library at Yale University.

Mitzel, J. (1972b). Entry May 30, 1972. MS 1779, John Mitzel Papers, Series IV: Diaries 1961-2002 Box 31 Folder 835. In. Beinecke Rare Book & Manuscript Library at Yale University.

Mitzel, J. (1972c). Entry June 25, 1972. MS 1779, John Mitzel Papers, Series IV: Diaries 1961-2002 Box 31 Folder 835. In. Beinecke Rare Book & Manuscript Library at Yale University.

Mitzel, J. (1973). Entry June 19, 1973. MS 1779, John Mitzel Papers, Series IV: Diaries 1961-2002 Box 31 Folder 837. In. Beinecke Rare Book & Manuscript Library at Yale University.

Mitzel, J. (1977a). Entry May 8, 1977. MS 1779, John Mitzel Papers, Series IV: Diaries 1961-2002 Box 32 Folder 849. In. Beinecke Rare Book & Manuscript Library at Yale University.

Mitzel, J. (1977b). Entry June 19, 1977. MS 1779, John Mitzel Papers, Series IV: Diaries 1961-2002 Box 32 Folder 849. In. Beinecke Rare Book & Manuscript Library at Yale University.

Mitzel, J. (1978a). Entry June 12, 1978. MS 1779, John Mitzel Papers, Series IV: Diaries 1961-2002 Box 32 Folder 852. In. Beinecke Rare Book & Manuscript Library at Yale University.

Mitzel, J. (1978b). Entry June 18, 1978. MS 1779, John Mitzel Papers, Series IV: Diaries 1961-2002 Box 32 Folder 852. In. Beinecke Rare Book & Manuscript Library at Yale University.

Mitzel, J. (February 12, 2012). *Interview with John Mitzel* [Interview]. https://www.youtube.com/watch?v=2C0HAnuK3j4

New England Gay Pride Week 1975: For Immediate Release. (June 13, 1975). In: The History Project Archives.

New England Gay Pride '76 Workshops. (1976). In: The History Project Archives.

Noble, E. (2021). *Stonewall Portraits: A Conversation with Elaine Noble* [Interview]. https://www.youtube.com/watch?v=8kqloL-WYj94

Parade Plans Bring Criticism. (May 25, 1974). *Gay Community News.*

Police again rout 'village' youths: Outbreak by 400 follows a near-riot over raid. (June 30, 1969). *New York Times.*

Project, T. H. Pride 1971. (n.d.) In: The History Project Archives.

Project, T. H. Pride 1973. (n.d.) In: The History Project Archives.

Project, T. H. Pride 1974 with Notes. (n.d.) In: The History Project Archives.

Project, T. H. Pride 1975. (n.d.) In: The History Project Archives.

Project, T. H. Pride 1976 with Notes. (n.d.) In: The History Project Archives.

Project, T. H. Pride 1977. (n.d.). In: The History Project Archives.

Project, T. H. Pride 1978. (n.d.). In: The History Project Archives.

Project, T. H. Pride 1979. (n.d.). In: The History Project Archives.

Rhino Files Suit. (June 22, 1974). *Gay Community News*.

Rhino Wins Grant. (May 11, 1974). *Gay Community News*.

Ridinger, R. B. (Ed.). (2004). *Speaking for Our Lives: Historic Speeches and Rhetoric for Gay and Lesbian Rights 1892-2000*. Harrington Park Press. Pg. 300

Ridinger, R. B. (Ed.). (2004). Pg. 314.

Riemer, M., & Brown, L. (2019). *We Are Everywhere: Protest, Power, and Pride in the History of Queer Liberation*. Ten Speed Press. Pg. 115

Riemer, M., & Brown, L. (2019). Pg. 140

Riemer, M., & Brown, L. (2019). Pg. 184-185

Sister Assaulted. (July 26, 1973). *Gay Community News*.

Stanley, J. (June 29, 2021). Upcoming Film 'Playland' Serves As Memorial To Boston's Lost LGBTQ Spaces. *WBUR.org* . https://www.wbur.org/news/2021/06/29/boston-lost-lgbtq-sp aces-playland-georden-west

Thorstad, D. (Ed.). (1976). *Gay Liberation and Socialism: Documents From the Discussions on Gay Liberation Inside the Socialist Workers Party (1970-1973)*.

Tobin, T. (April 28, 2002). Bankruptcy, ill will plague Bryant. *St. Petersburg Times*.

CHAPTER TWO NOTES

Adams, J. M. (June 12, 1988). Gay Pride Day: A community celebrates itself. *Boston Globe*.

AIDS Action Committee. (n.d.). *History of the AIDS Action Committee*. In. History Project Archives.

Ames, L. (1988). Letter: Pride Guide. In: The History Project Archives.

Bickelhaupt, S. (June 14, 1987). 30,000 gays rally to show pride, fight prejudice. *Boston Globe*.

Boston Common rally to highlight Gay Pride Month. (June 15, 1980). *Boston Globe*.

Bouvier, L., & Krone, M. (2015).

Bruni, S. (2019). Corporate responsibility makes prides go 'round. *Boston Pride Guide 2019*.

Burns, R., Crandall, N., & Rofes, E. (Eds.). (1980). *Gay Jubilee: A Guide book to Gay Boston, It's History and Resources*. Lesbian and Gay Taskforce of Jubilee 350.

Calendar of Events Pride 1980. (1980). In: The History Project Archives.

Cheevers, J. (December 26, 1982). Campaign begins to combat AIDS: Gay bartenders help provide information. *Boston Globe*.

Daley, J. (Ed.). (2010). *Great Speeches on Gay Rights* (Dover Thrift ed.). Dover Publications, Inc. Pg. 75.

Devall, C., & Marcus, J. (June 17, 1981). Gays protest Robin MacCormack layoff. *Boston Globe*.

Drogin, B. (November 10, 1988). How Presidential Race Was Won-Lost: Michael S. Dukakis. *Los Angeles Times*.

Goldsmith, L. (June 27, 1981). Community demonstrates against Mayor White over loss of liaison. *Gay Community News*.

Goldsmith, L. (July 4, 1981). City fails to alter Pride march. *Gay Community News*.

Goldsmith, L. (August 29, 1981). Boston promises reinstatement of liaison. *Gay Community News*.

Goldsmith, L. (June 19, 1982). Critics decry 'imbalance' in Pride plans. *Gay Community News*.

Goldsmith, L. (June 26, 1982). Mayor appoints Brian McNaught as new liaison. *Gay Community News*.

Goodridge et al v. Department of Public Health, (Massachusetts Supreme Judicial Court 2003).

Grady, D. (June 12, 1988). Thousands march to send a message of unity, strength. *Boston Globe*.

Guilfoy, C. (May 18, 1985). State removes children from gay foster parents. *Gay Community News*.

Guilfoy, C. (June 8, 1985). Outrage grows against gay foster policy. *Gay Community News*.

The History Project. *Home.* (n.d.). https://www.historyproject.org

HIV.gov. *A Timeline of HIV/AIDS.* https://files.hiv.gov/s3fs-public/aidsgov-timeline.pdf

Holder, A. (April 27, 1985). Conflict builds over gay pride day planning. *Gay Community News*.

Howe, P. J. (June 11, 1989). Thousands rally for gay pride: Showing their pride festivities blend with AIDS concern. *Boston Globe*.

InterPride. (August 11, 2021). The History of InterPride. *Medium*. https://medium.com/interpride/the-history-of-interpride-3ab8a4de9a49

Langner, P. (November, 17, 1983). A Look at the Boston City Council; David Scondras. *Boston Globe*.

Ledgard, L. (June 19, 1983). 18,000 march in Hub for lesbian, gay pride. *Boston Globe*.

Macias, A. (June 15, 1986). Marchers express solidarity at Gay Pride parade: Gay Pride. *Boston Globe*.

Marcus, J. (June 10, 1981). Gays, lesbians vow march on mayoral aide's dismissal. *Boston Globe*.

Mitzel, J. (1981). Entry June 24, 1981. MS 1779, John Mitzel Papers, Series IV: Diaries 1961-2002 Box 32 Folder 856. In. Beinecke Rare Book & Manuscript Library at Yale University.

Mitzel, J. (1982). Entry June 20, 1982. MS 1779, John Mitzel Papers, Series IV: Diaries 1961-2002 Box 32 Folder 857. In. Beinecke Rare Book & Manuscript Library at Yale University.

Mitzel, J. (1983). Entry May 21, 1983. MS 1779, John Mitzel Papers, Series IV: Diaries 1961-2002 Box 32 Folder 859. In. Beinecke Rare Book & Manuscript Library at Yale University.

Mitzel, J. (1984). Entry June 16, 1984. MS 1779, John Mitzel Papers, Series IV: Diaries 1961-2002 Box 32 Folder 860. In. Beinecke Rare Book & Manuscript Library at Yale University.

Mitzel, J. (1986). Entry June 9, 1986. MS 1779, John Mitzel Papers, Series IV: Diaries 1961-2002 Box 32 Folder 837. In. Beinecke Rare Book & Manuscript Library at Yale University.

Morris, D. (June 13, 1981). Liaison position axed. *Gay Community News*.

Murphy, S., & Anand, G. (June 20, 1995). US decision is hailed in South Boston. *Boston Globe*.

New Boston Pride Committee, I. (2019). Boston Pride Guide. In (Vol. 5, pp. 172): Boston Pride.

Noble, E. (2021).

Pane, L. M. (June 17, 1984). 15,000 join Boston march for gay rights. *Boston Globe*.

Pride Celebrations, Inc. (1985). Fifteen Years of Pride: The History and Purpose of Pride. In: Northeastern University Archives and Special Collections.

Program of Events for "the March" of Pride Fest '88. (1988). In: The History Project Archives.

Project, T. H. Pride 1982. (n.d.) In: The History Project Archives.

Project, T. H. Pride 1983. (n.d.). In: The History Project Archives.

Project, T. H. Pride 1984. (n.d.). In: The History Project Archives.

Project, T. H. Pride 1985. (n.d.). In: The History Project Archives.

Project, T. H. Pride 1986. (n.d.). In: The History Project Archives.

Project, T. H. Pride 1987. (n.d.). In: The History Project Archives.

Ribadeniera, D. (October 7, 1997). Foster ruling stands up State placed boy in gay household. *Boston Globe*.

Ridinger, R. B. (Ed.). (2004). Pg. 466

Ridinger, R. B. (Ed.). (2004). Pg. 469

Ridinger, R. B. (Ed.). (2004). Pg. 473

Rights groups blast policy against gay foster parents. (May 28, 1985). *Boston Globe*.

Rubin, E. (June 22, 1980). 5000, 'gay and proud,' march for their rights. *Boston Globe*.

Sipress, A. (June 20, 1982). Gays hold parade, rally in Boston. *Boston Globe*.

Weir, J. (August 23, 1994). Mad about the boys: What is the story behind NAMBLA? Our writer visits the boy lovers' summer convention. *Advocate*.

Witcher, G. (June 8, 1984). 400 homosexuals rally, mark gay pride week in Boston. *Boston Globe*.

CHAPTER THREE NOTES

1993 Boston Gay & Lesbian Pride Week: Calendar of Events. (1993). In. The History Project Archives.

Abraham, Y. (June 13, 1999). Tinky Winky a favorite in Gay Pride parade. *Boston Globe*.

ADMIN. (10/5/2010). Power: The Straight Scoop on Thirty-Five Gay Power Players. *Boston Magazine*.

Allied War Veterans Council. (n.d.). *The Parade's History*. https://southbostonparade.org/history/

Aucoin, D. (March 5, 1992). Gays may sue organizers over St. Patrick's parade ban. *Boston Globe*.

Aucoin, D. (March 6, 1992). Gays offer to limit their parade role. *Boston Globe*.

Aucoin, D. (March 12, 1992). Judge lets gays march in parade South Boston group won't appeal. *Boston Globe*.

Aucoin, D. (March 13, 1992). Concerned for safety, five groups quit parade. *Boston Globe*.

Aucoin, D., & Dabilis, A. (March 16, 1992). Jeers, threats greet gays in South Boston parade. *Boston Globe*.

Aucoin, D., & Anand, G. (June 12, 1996). Lewd acts decried in gay march. *Boston Globe*.

Biography.com. (October 12, 2022). *Andrew Cunanan*. https://www.biography.com/crime/andrew-cunanan

Boston Gay Pride, Inc. (1994). Proposed Budget for Gay Pride. In: The History Project Archives.

Bouvier, L., & Krone, M. (2015).

Briggs, L. (June 17-23, 1990). Boston Pride at 20. *Gay Community News*.

Clegg, E. (June 23, 1996). Q&A with the co-chairs of the Pride Committee. *Boston Globe*.

Diaz, J. (June 10, 1995). Gay 'Pride 1995' set to glitter for its silver anniversary. *Boston Globe*.

Dowdy, Z. R. (March 20, 1995). Gay would-be marchers hold a party, along with hopes for a berth in '96. *Boston Globe*.

The Dyke March Committee (June 1996). *To the community*

The Dyke March Committee (1996). *Post Bedgate Letter* http://bostondykemarcharchive.weebly.com/uploads/7/0/2/5/7025237/post_bed_letter_n_poem_96.pdf

Ellement, J., & Black, C. (March 12, 1994). SJC says gays may march in parade Veterans threaten to cancel event. *Boston Globe*.

Epperly, J. (June 13, 1996). Gross stupidity at a great parade. *Bay Windows*. http://bostondykemarcharchive.weebly.com/uploads/7/0/2/5/7025237/bay_june_13_c_sm.pdf

Fainaru, S. (June 26, 1994). Gays recall landmark protest New York riot 25 years ago 'outed' the movement. *Boston Globe*.

Giampetruzzi, T. (2001). Back on track: After years of mounting obstacles, Boston Pride regains its footing. *2001 New England Pride Guide*.

HIV.gov. (n.d.)

Janules, H. (1996). *For those who didn't get it: Bedgate, 1996*

John J. Hurley and South Boston Allied War Veterans Council v. Irish-American Gay, Lesbian and Bisexual Group of Boston, etc., et al., (Supreme Court of the United States 1995).

Keegan, R. (July 1996). Controversy over Pride: Whose community is it? *Sojourner*.

Kiehl, S. (June 15, 1998). 150 Marchers celebrate gay pride in Lawerence. *Boston Globe*.

Lakshmanan, I. A. R. (March 20, 1995). S. Boston parade, already protesting gay group, bars veterans with AIDS. *Boston Globe*.

Leung, S. (June 13, 1996). Pride parade organizers vow to end lewdness. *Boston Globe*.

Longcope, K. (June 1990). 70,000 rally for gay pride. *Boston Globe*.

Longcope, K. (June 9, 1991). Proud to march 90,000 turn out at parade to celebrate strides made by gays, lesbians. *Boston Globe*.

Lopez, R. (2019). Pg. 269.

Martinez, A. (June 11, 1995). Celebrating 25 years of Gay Pride. *Boston Globe*.

Migliori, L. (March 9, 1997). Boston Pride committee's guiding light: Sabrina Taylor. *In Newsweekly*.

Mont, J. (June 18-24, 1996). Pride and prejudice: Parade controversy creates rift among gay activists. *The Tab*. http://bostondykemarcharchive.weebly.com/uploads/7/0/2/5/7025237/tab_june_18_1996.pdf

Mont, J. (June 25-July 1, 1996). Clash takes place among gay leaders: Powerful political divisions bared in wake of parade. *The Tab*. http://bostondykemarcharchive.weebly.com/uploads/7/0/2/5/7025237/tab_july_1_1996.pdf

Murphy, S., & Anand, G. (June 20, 1995).

Nangeroni, N. (1994). *Boston Pride Speech June 1994*. http://www.gendertalk.com/pride/

Nangeroni, N. (1998). *Boston Pride Speech June 1998*. http://www.gendertalk.com/pride-98/

Nealon, P. (November 11, 1993). S. Boston parade sponsors ordered to supply data. *Boston Globe*.

No room on the stage? (July 1997).

O'Brien, E. (June 8, 1997). 100,000 march to celebrate Hub's Gay Pride event goes off with humor, teasing, community spirit. *Boston Globe*.

Outwords. *Outwords Archive: Nancy Nangeroni*. Retrieved September 20, 2024 from https://theoutwordsarchive.org/interview/nangeroni-nancy/

Pliner, E., & Taylor, S. (1998). Letter: Boston Pride 1998. In: The History Project Archives.

Pride. (May 1999). *The Boston Phoenix*.

Pride 1996 Calendar of Events. (1996). In: The History Project Archives.

The Pride Committee, Inc. (1993). *1993 Form 990*. In. The History Project Archives.

Project, T. H. Pride 1991. In. The History Project Archives.

Project, T. H. Pride 1992. In. The History Project Archives.

Project, T. H. Pride 1994. In: The History Project Archives.

Project, T. H. Pride 1995. In: The History Project Archives.

Project, T. H. Pride 1996. In: The History Project Archives.

Puga, A. (June 20, 1995). high court says veterans can bar gays from parade Speech rights at issue in St. Patrick's event. *Boston Globe*.

Retro Pride Boston 1998: Calendar of Events. (1998). In: The History Project Archives.

Rezendes, M. (March 18, 1992). Flynn decries heckling of gays Vows to support new march bids. *Boston Globe*.

Rezendes, M. (March 14, 1994). Would-be marchers rap city Gay group grumbles at mayor's lack of contingency parade plan. *Boston Globe*.

Rimer, S. (December 4, 2019). Opening Doors: John Ward. *Bostonia*. https://www.bu.edu/articles/2019/a-career-spent-fighting-for-the-rights-of-lgbtq-individuals/#comments

Ring, T. (May 14, 2022). Urvashi Vaid, Legendary Activist for LGBTQ+ Civil Rights, Dies at 63. *Advocate*. https://www.advocate.com/news/2022/5/14/legendary-activist-urvashi-vaid-dies-63

Scott, G. *Gunner Scott*. Retrieved September 20, 2024 from https://about.me/gunnerscott

Secretary of the Commonwealth of Massachusetts. (1990). *Corporation Master Display: Lavender Rhino, Inc.*

Taylor, J. (April 5, 1998). Permit request for gay march in Lawerence evokes debate. *Boston Globe*.

Walker, A. (January 7, 1993). Veterans ask court to halt gays' hearing on parade. *Boston Globe*.

Wong, D. S. (February 20, 1993). Gays win OK to join parade Sponsors ordered to liftSt. Pat's ban. *Boston Globe*.

CHAPTER FOUR NOTES

9/11 Memorial & Museum. *9/11 Primer*. Retrieved June 21, 2024 from https://www.911memorial.org/learn/resources/911-primer

Abel, D. (June 11, 2000). Gays hush their critics at parade. *Boston Globe*.

Abel, D. (May 24, 2004). Romney is booed at Suffolk commencement Governor's opposition to gay marriage spurs criticism and protest. *Boston Globe*.

Abraham, Y. (May 16, 2004). On the eve of gay marriage for one couple, joy is mixed with worry. *Boston Globe*.

Anonymous. (April 13, 2010). Looking Back. *Boston Globe*.

Black Lives Matter Protesters (June 13, 2015). A Statement from Boston Pride Parade Protesters. *Bay Windows*.

BoardSource. (2016). Term Limits: Thumbs Up? Thumbs Down?

Boston Dyke March Committee (2007). *Statement by Boston Dyke March Committee: Read from the Dyke March stage the night of 2007   Dyke   March* http://bostondykemarcharchive.weebly.com/uploads/7/0/2/5/7025237/6._statement_by_boston_dyke_march_committee.pdf

Boston Dyke March Committee (June 2007). *Website Statement Addressing Ongoing Controversy over Cancellation of Bitch's Performance* http://bostondykemarcharchive.weebly.com/uploads/7/0/2/5/7025237/7._dmc_statement_address_controver.pdf

Bouvier, L., & Krone, M. (2015).

Bruni, S. (2019).

Burge, K. (July 15, 2003). SJC puts off a decision on gay marriage. *Boston Globe*.

Davis, A. (2004). Welcome to Boston Pride 2004. *Boston Pride Guide 2004*.

Editorial. (January 3, 2007). A shameful reversal of rights. *Boston Globe*.

The gay agenda: Pride 2001. (June 7, 2001). *Boston Globe*.

Goodridge, T. (2016). Black Lives Matter Timeline. In. Georgetown University Library.

Goodridge et al v. Department of Public Health, (Massachusetts Supreme Judicial Court 2003).

IMDB.com. *Wilson Cruz*. Retrieved June 18, 2024 from https://www.imdb.com/name/nm0190497/

InterPride. *Conference*. Retrieved July 16, 2024 from https://www.interpride.org/conference/

John Geddes Lawrence and Tyron Garner, Petitioners v. Texas, (Supreme Court of the United States 2003).

LaTronica, M. (July 2002). Please, burst my bubble. *Sojourner*.

Levenson, M. (June 9, 2005). Patrick to march in Boston's gay parade; Reilly says he has prior commitment. *Boston Globe*.

Levenson, M. (September 30, 2006). Gay couple from R.I. win Mass. ruling; Superior Court Judge says longtime partners can marry. *Boston Globe*.

Levenson, M. (June 11, 2014). Democrats forced to choose: Pride or convention. *Boston Globe*.

Lewis, R. (May 16, 2005). Passage of marriage amendment in doubt. *Boston Globe*.

Lewis, R. (September 8, 2005). Reilly OK's 2008 initiative on ban of gay marriage. *Boston Globe*.

Lewis, R., & Abraham, Y. (May 20, 2004). Senate votes to end 1913 law action is tied to gay marriages. *Boston Globe*.

Lopez, R. (2019). Pg. 281.

McCabe, K. (January 22, 2013). Obama stuns with call for gay rights. *Boston Globe*.

Neff, L. (June 25, 2002). Pride by many other names. *The Advocate*.

New Boston Pride Committee, I. Float Documentation for Participation in the Parade.

New Boston Pride Committee, I. *FY 2000 Form 990*.

New Boston Pride Committee, I. *FY 2002 Form 990*.

New Boston Pride Committee, I. *FY 2004 Form 990*.

New Boston Pride Committee, I. *FY 2008 Form 990*.

New Boston Pride Committee, I. *FY 2011 Form 990*.

New Boston Pride Committee, I. *FY 2012 Form 990*.

New Boston Pride Committee, I. *FY 2016 Form 990*.

New Boston Pride Committee, I. *FY 2020 Form 990*.

New Boston Pride Committee, I. Parade Vehicle Inspection Criteria.

New Boston Pride Committee, I. *2019 Pride Marshals*. Retrieved June 18, 2024 from https://www.bostonpride.org/marshal/

New Boston Pride Committee, I. (2002). Welcome to Pride 2002. *2002 New England Pride Guide*.

New Boston Pride Committee, I. (2003). March Registration Form.

New Boston Pride Committee, I. (2006). Boston Pride Parade 2006: Group Marshal Handbook.

New Boston Pride Committee, I. (2006). Boston Pride Newsletter. In (Vol. 1 Issue 1).

New Boston Pride Committee, I. (2006). Boston Pride Newsletter. In (Vol. 1 Issue2).

New Boston Pride Committee, I. (June 7, 2006). *Statement of the Boston Pride Committee on Macy's Succumbing to Anti-Gay Sentiments* https://web.archive.org/web/20060619095938/http://www.boston-pride.org:80/MacysJune7.pdf

New Boston Pride Committee, I. (2007).

New Boston Pride Committee, I. (2008). *By-Laws*.

New Boston Pride Committee, I. (2010). InterPride 30th Anniversary Annual General Meeting Preliminary Bid.

New Boston Pride Committee, I. (March 13, 2012). Boston to host InterPride's 2012 Annual World Conference, celebrating its 30th Anniversary. https://www.boston-pride.org/2012/03/boston-to-host-interprides-2012-annu-al-world-conference-celebrating-its-30th-anniversary/

New Boston Pride Committee, I. (April 24, 2012). Boston Pride to Host InterPride Mid-Year Meeting. https://www.bostonpride.org/2012/04/boston-pride-to-host-in-terpride-mid-year-meeting/

New Boston Pride Committee, I. (May 31, 2012). DOMA declared unconstitutional. https://www.boston-pride.org/2012/05/doma-declared-unconstitutional/

New Boston Pride Committee, I. (May 1, 2013). Boston Pride announces first ever Pride Night @ Fenway Park! https://www.bostonpride.org/2013/05/boston-pride-an-nounces-first-ever-pride-night-fenway-park/

Obama, B. (January 20, 2013). *Inaugural Address by President Barack Obama* https://obamawhitehouse.archives.gov/the-press-office/2013/01/21/inaugural-address-president-barack-obama

Reed, J. (June 3, 2004). Gay Pride heads to the chapel of love. *Boston Globe*.

Russell, J. (June 9, 2002). Parents, families celebrate gay pride. *Boston Globe*.

Straw, J., Ford, B., & McShane, L. (April 17, 2013). Police narrow in on two suspects in Boston Marathon bombing. *The Daily News*.

Sudborough, S. (June 22, 2022). Rita Hester's murder and legacy are important to Boston, so she's getting a mural in Allston. *Boston.com*.

Tench, M. (June 15, 2003). Message-laden march puts politics, gay pride on parade. *Boston Globe*.

Tench, M. (May 16, 2004). Wedding option energizes teenagers at youth pride rally. *Boston Globe*.

Trigilio, J. *Political Context: Controversy over scheduled Bitch performance at the 2007 Dyke March* [Interview]. http://bostondykemarcharchive.weebly.com/uploads/7/0/2/5/7025237/1._bitch_political_context.pdf

Ulloa, J. (June 14, 2009). Pride Parade mourns loss of longtime leader. *Boston Globe*.

Valencia, M. (December 8, 2012). High court takes on gay marriage case. *Boston Globe*.

Vennochi, J. (June 14, 2007). Marriage debate is a test of Patrick's power. *Boston Globe*.

Wangsness, L. (June 8, 2007). Patrick to join march for gay pride. *Boston Globe*.

Woolhouse, M. (June 13, 2010). Boston's gay pride parade goes marching through the rain. *Boston Globe*.

Yee, V. (June 12, 2011). Rain doesn't dampen pride parade. *Boston Globe*.

CHAPTER FIVE NOTES

Abad-Santos, A. (June 25, 2018). How LGBTQ Pride Month became a branded holiday. *VOX*.

Alvarez, L., & Kenny, S. (June 13, 2016). At least 50 dead after attack at U.S. nightclub; Florida assault is being investigated as terrorism after police kill gunman. *New York Times*.

Andersen, T. (February 19, 2021). Boston Pride cancels 2021 parade due to coronavirus. *Boston Globe*.

Annear, S. (April 4, 2016). Boston Pride un invites parade marshal over online remarks. *Boston Globe*.

Black Lives Matter Protestors (June 13, 2015).

Boston Pride Communications Committee. (2020). *Original Statement on Black and Brown Violence by Police*

Boston Pride Volunteers. (2020). Many volunteers of Boston Pride's workforce ask board to resign. In I. New Boston Pride Committee (Ed.). pride4thepeople.org.

Browne, R., Lee, A., & Rigdon, R. (June 1, 2020). There are as many National Guard members activated in the US as there are active duty troops in Iraq, Syria and Afghanistan. *CNN*. https://www.cnn.com/2020/06/01/us/national-guard-pr otests-states-map-trnd/index.html

Bruni, S. (2019).

Cole, A. (July 10, 2020). Boston Pride board resignation sought, new org. says. *Rainbow Times*.

Ebbert, S. (December 29, 2020). Boycott Boston Pride, say activists who bolted for social justice. *Boston Globe*.

Ebbert, S. (January 2, 2021). Activists call for boycott of Boston Pride celebration. *Boston Globe*.

Ebbert, S. (June 2, 2021). LGBTQ activists upstage mayoral forum by Boston Pride. *Boston Globe*.

Ebbert, S. (June 9, 2021). Transforming Boston Pride. *Boston Globe*.

Ebbert, S. (June 10, 2021). Boycott brings change to Boston Pride leadership. *Boston Globe*.

Fitzsimmons, T. (June 12, 2018). What really happened that night at Pulse. *NBC News*. https://www.nbcnews.com/feature/nbc-out/what-really-happened-night-pulse-n882571

GLBTQ Legal Advocates & Defenders. (May 11, 2021).

Graham, R. (July 5, 2019). 'Pride' is not just a marketing opportunity. *Boston Globe*.

Goodridge, T. (2016).

Hessekiel, D. (July 25, 2019). Should Corporations Participate Loudly In Pride? *Forbes*.

Hiliard, J., Wu, S., MacQuarrie, B., & Ortiz, A. (August 31, 2019). Protesters jee rStraight Pride Parade marchers along route to City Hall. *Boston Globe*.

Hill, E., Tiefenthaler, A., Triebert, C., Jordan, D., Willis, H., & Stein, R. (May 31, 2020). How George Floyd Was Killed in Police Custody. *New York Times*. https://www.nytimes.com/2020/05/31/us/george-floyd-investigation.html

Hoover, A. (April 4, 2016). Boston Pride withdraws invitation to police officer to serve as parade marshal. *Boston.com*. https://www.boston.com/news/local-news/2016/04/04/boston-pride-withdraws-invitation-to-police-officer-to-serve-as-parade-marshal/

Kearnan, S. (June 6, 2020). Boston Pride's response to the Black Lives Matter protests is a shame. *Boston Magazine*.

Kekatos, M. (March 11, 2024). COVID-19 timeline: How the deadly virus and the world's response have evolved over 4 years. *ABC News*. https://abcnews.go.com/Health/covid-19-timeline-deadly-virus-worlds-response-evolved/story?id=107880313

LePore, S. (December 31, 2023). Former Biden head of nuclear waste policy Sam Brinton ends 2023 a FREE person after being accused of stealing women's clothing from airport suitcases. *Dai-

ly Mail.https://www.dailymail.co.uk/news/article-12915165/Sa m-Brinton-Biden-official-free-2023.html

Mason, A. (June 10, 2016).

Meyer, M. (October 13, 2021). The Implosion of Boston's Pride Parade is a Sign of Things to Come. *Quillette*. https://quillette.com/2021/10/13/the-implo-sion-of-bostons-pride-parade-is-a-sign-of-things-to-come/

Monroe, R. I. *About Irene Monroe*. Retrieved August 20, 2024 from https://www.irenemonroe.com/about/

Monroe, R. I. (June 20, 2018). What's happening to Pride? *Windy City Times*.

Monroe, R. I. (November 8, 2021). Why shut down Boston Pride? Racism is not the only reason for the closure. *Boston Spirit Maga-zine*.

TheNetwork/LA Red. (February 2021).

New Boston Pride Committee, I. *FY 2015 Form 990*.

New Boston Pride Committee, I. *FY 2017 Form 990*.

New Boston Pride Committee, I. *FY 2020 Form 990*.

New Boston Pride Committee, I. (October 8, 2014). Boston Pride Launches Its Own Official Pride Guide in 2015. https://www.bostonpride.org/2014/10/boston-pride-launch-es-its-own-official-pride-guide-in-2015/

New Boston Pride Committee, I. (2015). Boston Pride Guide. In (Vol. 1): Sylvain Bruni.

New Boston Pride Committee, I. (2015). *2015 Boston Pride Gala*. Retrieved July 27, 2024 from http://web.archive.org/web/20150 609022709/https://www.bostonpride.org/gala/

New Boston Pride Committee, I. (May 12, 2015). Boston Pride Will Kick Off Pride Week and 45th Anniversary with First Ever G a l a .   h t t p s : / / w w w . b o s t o n -

pride.org/2015/05/boston-pride-will-kick-off-pride-week-and-45th-anniversary-with-first-ever-gala/

New Boston Pride Committee, I. (June 16, 2015). Boston Pride Thanks Community for Successful 45th Annual Celebration. h t t p s : / / w w w . b o s t o n - pride.org/2015/06/boston-pride-thanks-community-for-successful-45th-annual-pride-week/

New Boston Pride Committee, I. (November 1, 2015). Introducing the Boston Pride Community Fund. https://www.bostonpride.org/2015/11/introducing-the-boston-pride-community-fund/

New Boston Pride Committee, I. (2016). Solidarity through Pride: With a commitment to community building, Boston Pride introduces two new programs. In. Boston Pride Guide 2016.

New Boston Pride Committee, I. (April 4, 2016). Boston Pride Statement Regarding Withdrawal of Parade Marshal. https://www.bostonpride.org/2016/04/boston-pride-statement-regarding-withdrawal-of-parade-marshal/

New Boston Pride Committee, I. (June 12, 2016). Boston Pride statement on the Orlando massacre. https://www.bostonpride.org/2016/06/boston-pride-statement-on-the-orlando-massacre/

New Boston Pride Committee, I. (July 1, 2016). A Look Back on Boston Pride Month 2016, Celebrations and Remembrances for the LGBT Community. h t t p s : / / w w w . b o s t o n - pride.org/2016/07/a-look-back-on-boston-pride-month-2016-celebrations-and-remembrances-for-the-lgbt-community/

New Boston Pride Committee, I. (June 29, 2017). Boston Pride attends World Pride 2017 in Madrid,

Spain. https://www.bostonpride.org/2017/06/boston-pride-at-tends-world-pride-2017-in-madrid-spain/

New Boston Pride Committee, I. (December 5, 2017). Boston Pride VP Linda DeMarco elected co-president of InterPride. https://www.bostonpride.org/2017/12/boston-pride-vp-linda-de-marco-elected-co-president-of-interpride/

New Boston Pride Committee, I. (2018). Boston Pride 2019 Partner-ship Packet.

New Boston Pride Committee, I. (December 18, 2018). Boston Pride Names Two New Board Members. https://www.boston-pride.org/2018/12/boston-pride-names-two-new-board-mem-bers/?ref=quillette.com

New Boston Pride Committee, I. (2019). Boston Pride Guide. In (Vol. 5): Boston Pride.

New Boston Pride Committee, I. (2019). 2019 Parade Line Up in Alpha Order.

New Boston Pride Committee, I. (2019a).

New Boston Pride Committee, I. (August 26, 2019). *Statement by Boston Pride Regarding Straight Pride*. https://web.archive.org/web/20190902140533/https://www.boston-pride.org/2019/08/statement-by-boston-pride-regard-ing-straight-pride/

New Boston Pride Committee, I. (2020). *Boston Pride Reworked Statement on Black and Brown Police Violence*

New Boston Pride Committee, I. (2020a). *#BlackLivesMatter*

New Boston Pride Committee, I. (2020c). *Letter to Our Community*

New Boston Pride Committee, I. (2020d). Trademark: Cease and Desist. In C. D. Henry Paquin, Jo Trigilio, Valerie Bee (Ed.). pr ide4thepeople.org.

New Boston Pride Committee, I. (2020e). Transformation Advisory Committee.

Nilsson, C. (June 6, 2023). The Rise, Fall, and Hopeful Return of Boston's Pride Parade. *Boston Magazine*. https://www.bostonmagazine.com/news/2023/06/06/boston-pride-parade-back/

Obergefell v. Hodges, 651 (2015). https://www.supreme-court.gov/opinions/boundvolumes/576BV.pdf#page=696

Pennington, J., Mulvihill, M., & Phelps, R. (May 25, 2023). The (R) Evolution of Boston Pride: How a grassroots group took over the Bay State's biggest LGBTQ+ event. *Boston Spirit Magazine*. https://bostonspiritmagazine.com/2023/05/the-revolution-of-boston-pride-how-a-grassroots-group-took-over-the-bay-states-biggest-lgbtq-event/

Phelps, R. (June 25, 2020). Boston Pride engages consultants to work on diversity and inclusion. *Boston Spirit Magazine*.

Phelps, R. (July 2, 2020). Tensions mount between Boston Pride and activists calling for board to resign. *Boston Spirit Magazine*.

Quinn, T., & Meiners, E. (July 29, 2015). Good cop? Bad cop? No cop! Queer resistance to policing. *Windy City Times*.

The Rainbow Times (June 9, 2018). Queer & Trans PoC Elevate Concerns of Systemic Racism at Boston Pride Parade. *The Rainbow Times*. https://www.therainbowtimesmass.com/queer-trans-poc-elevate-concerns-of-systemic-racism-at-boston-pride-parade/?ref=quillette.com

The Rainbow Times. (July 9, 2021). Boston Pride dissolves after pressure. *The Rainbow Times*.

Salinas, S. (June 11, 2017). A celebration of Pride, with a tinge of mourning. *Boston Globe*.

Shanahan, M. (June 9, 2017). Boston Pride apologizes for Facebook post. *Boston Globe*.

Sweeney, E. (June 26, 2019). Boston officials approve 'Straight Pride Parade' application; event to be held Aug 31. *Boston Globe*.

Trans Resistance MA. *About the Resistance*. Retrieved August 22, 2024 from https://www.transresistancema.com/about

Trigilio, J. (2022). *Interview* [Interview].

Wang, V., & Allen, E. (June 11, 2016). Boston's Pride Parade was a celebration, and a statement. *Boston Globe*.

AFTERWARD NOTES

@jacques_cabaret. (June 8, 2024). *We at Jacques would like to publicly apologize for leaving a f*ck*ng bus in the middle of the parade. We intended to ride it to the finish line, but it broke down and we evacuated like it was d*mn Titanic. We hope the city of Boston can forgive us in time, but in the meantime, please come to our shows today at 3pm, 7pm, and 10pm. Happy Pride.* X.

Boston Spirit Magazine. Former Boston Pride president named US Association of Prides hall of famer. (January 31, 2023). *Boston Spirit   Magazine*. https://bostonspiritmagazine.com/2023/01/former-boston-pride-president-named-us-association-of-prides-hall-of-famer/

Cotter, S. (June 8, 2024). Boston Pride parade awash in positivity. *Boston Globe*. https://www.bostonglobe.com/2024/06/08/metro/boston-pride-parade/

Doan-Nguyen, R. (June 28, 2022). 'The End of One Era': Marching Toward a New Boston Pride. *Harvard Crimson*. https://www.thecrimson.com/article/2022/6/28/boston-pride-dissolved/

Eberwein, E. (June 6, 2024). Activist groups demand 'no pride in genocide' ahead of Boston Pride parade. *WGBH*.

https://www.wgbh.org/news/local/2024-06-06/activist-groups-demand-no-pride-in-genocide-ahead-of-boston-pride-parade

Eberwein, E. (June 8, 2024). Celebration and protest mark Boston Pride parade. *WGBH*. https://www.wgbh.org/news/local/2024-06-08/celebration-and-protest-mark-boston-pride-parade

Gabrault, Emily, Assistant Attorney General. Re: Your Public Records Request. In D. Gonzalez (Ed.).

GLBTQ Legal Advocates & Defenders. (July 12, 2021). *GLAD Responds to Boston Pride Board's Dissolution Announcement* https://www.glad.org/post/glad-responds-to-boston-pride-boards-dissolution-announcement/

Fenway Health. *Adrianna Boulin*. Retrieved August 20, 2024 from https://fenwayhealth.org/leadership-committee/adrianna-boulin/

Liberate Boston Pride. (June 7, 2024). *A letter to Boston Pride for the People from 67 organizations* https://liberatebostonpride.wordpress.com

Loesch, C. (June 2, 2023). Boston Pride Returns After Controversy And COVID Forced A 3-Year Halt. *Patch.com*. https://patch.com/massachusetts/boston/boston-pride-returns-after-controversy-covid-forced-3-year-halt

Monroe, R. I. (November 8, 2021).

Monroe, R. I. (June 16, 2022). Moving beyond Boston Pride with Pop-Up Pride on Boston Common. *Boston Spirit Magazine*. https://bostonspiritmagazine.com/2022/06/moving-beyond-boston-pride-with-pop-up-boston-pride-on-the-common/

Nilsson, C. (June 6, 2023).

No Pinkwashing Boston.(June 21, 2023). *Boston Rejects Zionist Pinkwashing* https://nopinkwashingboston.wordpress.com

Pennington, J., Mulvihill, M., & Phelps, R. (May 25, 2023).

Phelps, R. (July 9, 2021).

The Rainbow Times. (July 9, 2021).

BIBLIOGRAPHY

4 policemen hurt in 'village' raid: Melee near Sheridan Square follows action at bar. (June 29, 1969). *New York Times*.

600 gay persons march in Boston observance. (June 23, 1974). *Boston Globe*.

9/11 Memorial & Museum. *9/11 Primer*. Retrieved June 21, 2024 from https://www.911memorial.org/learn/resources/911-primer

1993 Boston Gay & Lesbian Pride Week: Calendar of Events. (1993). In. The History Project Archives.

Abad-Santos, A. (June 25, 2018). How LGBTQ Pride Month became a branded holiday. *VOX*.

Abel, D. (June 11, 2000). Gays hush their critics at parade. *Boston Globe*.

Abel, D. (May 24, 2004). Romney is booed at Suffolk commencement Governor's opposition to gay marriage spurs criticism and protest. *Boston Globe*.

Abraham, Y. (June 13, 1999). Tinky Winky a favorite in Gay Pride parade. *Boston Globe*.

Abraham, Y. (May 16, 2004). On the eve of gay marriage for one couple, joy is mixed with worry. *Boston Globe*.

Adams, J. M. (June 12, 1988). Gay Pride Day: A community celebrates itself. *Boston Globe*.

ADMIN. (October 5, 2010). Power: The Straight Scoop on Thirty-Five Gay Power Players. *Boston Magazine*.

AIDS Action Committee. (n.d.). *History of the AIDS Action Committee*. In. History Project Archives.

Allied War Veterans Council. (n.d.). *The Parade's History*. https://southbostonparade.org/history/

Alvarez, L.,& Kenny, S. (June 13, 2016). At least 50 dead after attack at U.S.nightclub; Florida assault is being investigated as terrorism after police kill gunman. *New York Times*.

Ames, L. (1988). Letter: Pride Guide. In: The History Project Archives.

Andersen, T. (February 19, 2021). Boston Pride cancels 2021 parade due to coronavirus. *Boston Globe*.

Annear, S. (April 4, 2016). Boston Pride un invites parade marshal over online remarks. *Boston Globe*.

Anonymous. (April 13, 2010). Looking Back. *Boston Globe*.

Aucoin, D. (March 5, 1992). Gays may sue organizers over St. Patrick's parade ban. *Boston Globe*.

Aucoin, D. (March 6, 1992). Gays offer to limit their parade role. *Boston Globe*.

Aucoin, D. (March 12, 1992). Judge lets gays march in parade South Boston group won't appeal. *Boston Globe*.

Aucoin, D. (March 13, 1992). Concerned for safety, five groups quit parade. *Boston Globe*.

Aucoin, D., & Dabilis, A. (March 16, 1992). Jeers, threats greet gays in South Boston parade. *Boston Globe*.

Aucoin, D., & Anand, G. (June 12, 1996). Lewd acts decried in gay march. *Boston Globe*.

Besen, W. (December 7, 2022). Has Sam Brinton's story always been too good to be true? *LGBTQ Nation*. https://www.lgbtqnation.com/2022/12/sam-brintons-story-always-good-true/

Bickelhaupt, S. (June 14, 1987). 30,000 gays rally to show pride, fight prejudice. *Boston Globe*.

Biography.com. (October 12, 2022). *Andrew Cunanan*. https://www.biography.com/crime/andrew-cunanan

Black Lives Matter Protesters (June 13, 2015). A Statement from Boston Pride Parade Protesters. *Bay Windows*.

BoardSource. (2016). Term Limits: Thumbs Up? Thumbs Down?

Boston Common rally to highlight Gay Pride Month. (June 15, 1980). *Boston Globe*.

Boston Dyke March Committee (2007). *Statement by Boston Dyke March Committee: Read from the Dyke March stage the night of 2007 Dyke March* http://bostondykemarcharchive.weebly.com/uploads/7/0/2/5/7025237/6._statement_by_boston_dyke_march_committee.pdf

Boston Dyke March Committee (June 2007). *Website Statement Addressing Ongoing Controversy over Cancellation of Bitch's Performance* http://bostondykemarcharchive.weebly.com/uploads/7/0/2/5/7025237/7._dmc_statement_address_controver.pdf

Boston Gay Pride, Inc. (1994). Proposed Budget for Gay Pride. In: The History Project Archives.

Boston Globe. *Lois Johnson Obituary*. Retrieved September 20, 2024 from https://www.legacy.com/us/obituaries/bostonglobe/name/lois-johnson-obituary?id=6791182

Boston Police indicted for extorting gay bars. (February 1988). *Campaign*.

Boston Pride Communications Committee. (2020). *Original Statement on Black and Brown Violence by Police*

Boston Pride Volunteers. (2020). Many volunteers of Boston Pride's workforce ask board to resign. In I. New Boston Pride Committee (Ed.). pride4thepeople.org.

Boston Spirit Magazine. Former Boston Pride president named US Association of Prides hall of famer. (January 31, 2023). *Boston Spirit Magazine*. https://bostonspiritmagazine.com/2023/01/former-boston-pride-president-named-us-association-of-prides-hall-of-famer/

Bouvier, L., & Krone, M. (2015). A history of Boston Pride. *Boston Pride Guide 2015 Supplement, 1*.

Briggs, L. (June 17-23, 1990). Boston Pride at 20. *Gay Community News*.

Bronski, M. *Shively, a Pivotal Figure in the Gay Liberation Movement*. Retrieved September 20, 2024 from https://lambdaliterary.org/2017/11/remembering-charles-shively/

Browne, R., Lee, A., & Rigdon, R. (June 1, 2020). There are as many National Guard members activated in the US as there are active duty troops in Iraq, Syria and Afghanistan. *CNN*. https://www.cnn.com/2020/06/01/us/national-guard-protests-states-map-trnd/index.html

Bruce, K. M.(2016). *Pride Parades: How a Parade Changed the World*. New York University Press.

Bruni, S. (2019). Corporate responsibility makes prides go 'round. *Boston Pride Guide 2019*.

Bumblebee, M. (June 12, 1976). "Unity" theme of Boston Gay Pride Week. *Gay Community News*.

Burge, K. (July 15, 2003). SJC puts off a decision on gay marriage. *Boston Globe*.

Burns, R., Crandall, N., & Rofes, E. (Eds.). (1980). *Gay Jubilee: A Guidebook to Gay Boston, It's History and Resources*. Lesbian and Gay Taskforce of Jubilee 350.

Calendar of Events Pride 1980. (1980). In: The History Project Archives.

Campbell, A. (2019). *Queer X Design: 50 Years of Signs, Symbols, Banners, Logos, and Graphic Art of LGBTQ*. Black Dog & Leventhal Publishers. Hatchette Book Group, Inc.

Centers for Disease Control (1981). *Morbidity and Mortality Weekly Report*, Morbidity and Mortality Weekly Report, Volume 30 Issue 21.

Cheevers, J. (December 26, 1982). Campaign begins to combat AIDS: Gay bartenders help provide information. *Boston Globe*.

Clegg, E. (June 23, 1996). Q&A with the co-chairs of the Pride Committee. *Boston Globe*.

Clendinen, D., & Nagourney, A. (1999). *Out for Good: The Struggle to Build a Gay Rights Movement in America*. Touchstone.

Cohen, A. The Boston/Boise Affair, 1977-78. (Essay). *The Gay & Lesbian Review Worldwide*.

Cole, A. (July 10, 2020). Boston Pride board resignation sought, new org. says. *Rainbow Times*.

Cotter, S. (June 8, 2024). Boston Pride parade awash in positivity. *Boston Globe*. https://www.bostonglobe.com/2024/06/08/metro/boston-pride-parade/

Daley, J. (Ed.). (2010). *Great Speeches on Gay Rights* (Dover Thrift ed.). Dover Publications, Inc.

Davis, A. (2004). Welcome to Boston Pride 2004. *Boston Pride Guide 2004*.

Devall, C., & Marcus, J. (June 17, 1981). Gays protest Robin Mac-Cormack layoff. *Boston Globe*.

Diaz, J. (June10, 1995). Gay 'Pride 1995' set to glitter for its silver anniversary. *Boston Globe*.

Dignify Boston (1977). Gay Pride '77. MS 1779, John Mitzel Papers, Series 1: Correspondence and Research Files 1962-2013 Box 6 Folder 259. In. Beinecke Rare Book & Manuscript Library at Yale University.

Doan-Nguyen, R. (June 28, 2022). 'The End of One Era': Marching Toward a New Boston Pride. *Harvard Crimson*. https://www.th ecrimson.com/article/2022/6/28/boston-pride-dissolved/

Dowdy, Z. R. (March 20, 1995). Gay would-be marchers hold a party, along with hopes for a berth in '96. *Boston Globe*.

Drogin, B. (November 10, 1988). How Presidential Race Was Won-Lost: Michael S. Dukakis. *Los Angeles Times*.

Durham, M. (December 31, 1971). Homosexuals in Revolt: The year that one liberation movement turned militant. *Life*.

Eastern Regional Conference of Homophile Organization (March 16, 1970). *Resolved*. In: Digital Collections of The History Project.

Ebbert, S. (June 30, 2020). Activists demand Pride board overhaul. *Boston Globe*.

Ebbert, S. (December 29, 2020). Boycott Boston Pride, say activists who bolted for social justice. *Boston Globe*.

Ebbert, S. (January 2, 2021). Activists call for boycott of Boston Pride celebration. *Boston Globe*.

Ebbert, S. (June 2, 2021). LGBTQ activists upstage mayoral forum by Boston Pride. *Boston Globe*.

Ebbert, S. (June 9, 2021). Transforming Boston Pride. *Boston Globe*.

Ebbert, S. (June 10, 2021). Boycott brings change to Boston Pride leadership. *Boston Globe*.

Eberwein, E. (June 6, 2024). Activist groups demand 'no pride in genocide' ahead of Boston Pride parade. *WGBH*.

https://www.wgbh.org/news/local/2024-06-06/ac-tivist-groups-demand-no-pride-in-geno-cide-ahead-of-boston-pride-parade

Eberwein, E. (June 8, 2024). Celebration and protest mark Boston Pride parade. *WGBH*. https://www.wgbh.org/news/local/2024-06-08/celebration-and-protest-mark-boston-pride-parade

Editorial. (January 3, 2007). A shameful reversal of rights. *Boston Globe*.

Eisenberg, D. (June 11, 2011). 41 years of Pride: It really has gotten better. *The Boston Phoenix*

Ellement, J., & Black, C. (March 12, 1994). SJC says gays may march in parade Veterans threaten to cancel event. *Boston Globe*.

Epperly, J. (June 13, 1996). Gross stupidity at a great parade. *Bay Windows*. http://bostondykemarcharchive.weebly.com/uploads/7/0/2/5/7025237/bay_june_13_c_sm.pdf

Fainaru, S. (June 26, 1994). Gays recall landmark protest New York riot 25 years ago 'outed' the movement. *Boston Globe*.

Fenway Health. *Adrianna Boulin*. Retrieved August 20, 2024 from https://fenwayhealth.org/leadership-committee/adrianna-boulin/

Fenway Muggings. (July 12, 1973). *Gay Community News*.

Fitzsimmons, T. (June 12, 2018). What really happened that night at Pulse. *NBC News*. https://www.nbcnews.com/feature/nbc-out/what-really-happened-night-pulse-n882571

Fosburgh, L. (June 29, 1970). Thousands of homosexuals hold a protest rally in Central Park. *New York Times*.

Gabrault, Emily, Assistant Attorney General. Re: Your Public Records Request. In D. Gonzalez (Ed.).

Gay Brother Murdered. (July 19,1973). *Gay Community News*.

Gay, Lesbian, Bisexual, and Transgender Historical Society. (n.d.). *Protests Independence Hall - Philadelphia, National - Homophile Organizations. July 1-4, 1965; n.d. TS Phyllis Lyon, Del Martin and the Daughters of Bilitis Box 20 Folder 32.*

Gay Pride Week: Come Celebrate With Us. (1971). In: The History Project Archives.

Gay Pride Week '72. (1972). In: The History Project Archives.

Gays Respond. (July 26, 1973). *Gay Community News.*

Gay rights supporters hold march. (June 17, 1979). *Boston Globe.*

Giampetruzzi, T. (2001). Back on track: After years of mounting obstacles, Boston Pride regains its footing. *2001 New England Pride Guide.*

GLBTQ Legal Advocates & Defenders. (May 11, 2021). *GLAD Supports Trans Resistance MA and Pride 4 the People in Calls for Transformation at Boston Pride* https://www.glad.org/post/glad-supports-calls-for-transformation-at-boston-pride/

GLBTQ Legal Advocates & Defenders. (July 12, 2021). *GLAD Responds to Boston Pride Board's Dissolution Announcement* https://www.glad.org/post/glad-responds-to-boston-pride-boards-dissolution-announcement/

Goldfarb, S. (July 28, 2010). *Sam Goldfarb talks about his most memorable Boston Pride* [Interview]. https://www.youtube.com/watch?v=yFnphpWvVDU

Goldsmith, L. (June 27, 1981). Community demonstrates against Mayor White over loss of liaison. *Gay Community News.*

Goldsmith, L. (July 4, 1981). City fails to alter Pride march. *Gay Community News.*

Goldsmith, L. (August 29, 1981). Boston promises reinstatement of liaison. *Gay Community News.*

Goldsmith, L. (June 19, 1982). Critics decry 'imbalance' in Pride plans. *Gay Community News*.

Goldsmith, L. (June 26, 1982). Mayor appoints Brian McNaught as new liaison. *Gay Community News*.

Goodridge et al v. Department of Public Health, (Massachusetts Supreme Judicial Court 2003).

Goodridge, T. (2016). Black Lives Matter Timeline. In. Georgetown University Library.

Grady, D. (June 12, 1988). Thousands march to send a message of unity, strength. *Boston Globe*.

Graham, R. (July 5, 2019). 'Pride' is not just a marketing opportunity. *Boston Globe*.

Guilfoy, C. (May 18, 1985). State removes children from gay foster parents. *Gay Community News*.

Guilfoy, C. (June 8, 1985). Outrage grows against gay foster policy. *Gay Community News*.

Hessekiel, D. (July 25, 2019). Should Corporations Participate Loudly In Pride? *Forbes*.

Hiliard, J., Wu, S., MacQuarrie, B., & Ortiz, A. (August 31, 2019). Protesters jeer Straight Pride Parade marchers along route to City Hall. *Boston Globe*.

Hill, E., Tiefenthaler, A., Triebert, C., Jordan, D., Willis, H., & Stein, R. (May 31, 2020). How George Floyd Was Killed in Police Custody. *New York Times*. https://www.nytimes.com/2020/05/31/us/george-floyd-investigation.html

HIV.gov.   (n.d.)   *A   Timeline   of   HIV/AIDS*. https://files.hiv.gov/s3fs-public/aidsgov-timeline.pdf

Holder, A. (April 27, 1985). Conflict builds over gay pride day planning. *Gay Community News*.

Hoover, A. (April 4, 2016). Boston Pride withdraws invitation to police officer to serve as parade marshal. *Boston.com*. https://www.boston.com/news/local-news/2016/04/04/boston -pride-withdraws-invitation-to-police-officer-to-serve-as-parade-m arshal/

Hostile crowd dispersed near Sheridan Square. (July 3, 1969). *New York Times*.

Howe, P. J. (June 11, 1989). Thousands rally for gay pride: Showing their pride Festivities blend with AIDS concern. *Boston Globe*.

IMDB.com. (n.d.). *Wilson Cruz*. Retrieved June 18,2024 from https://www.imdb.com/name/nm0190497/

InterPride. *Conference*. Retrieved July 16, 2024 from https://www.i nterpride.org/conference/

InterPride. (August 11, 2021). The History of InterPride. *Medium*. https://medium.com/interpride/the-history-of-inter-pride-3ab8a4de9a49

Janules, H. (1996). *For those who didn't get it: Bedgate, 1996*

John J. Hurley and South Boston Allied War Veterans Council v. Irish-American Gay, Lesbian and Bisexual Group of Boston, etc., et al., (Supreme Court of the United States 1995).

John Geddes Lawrence and Tyron Garner, Petitioners v. Texas, (Supreme Court of the United States 2003).

Johnson, I. (December 7, 1974). Lavender rhino at last on subway! *Gay Community News*.

Johnson, L. (July 27, 2010). *Lois Johnson talks about early Pride marches* [Interview]. https://www.youtube.com/watch?v=dKK_zt1oa8Q

Kearnan, S. (June 6, 2020). Boston Pride's response to the Black Lives Matter protests is a shame. *Boston Magazine*.

Keegan, R. (July 1996). Controversy over Pride: Whose community is it? *Sojourner*.

Kekatos, M. (March 11, 2024). COVID-19 timeline: How the deadly virus and the world's response have evolved over 4 years. *ABC News*. https://abcnews.go.com/Health/covid-19-timeline-deadly -virus-worlds-response-evolved/story?id=107880313

Kiehl, S. (June 15, 1998). 150 Marchers celebrate gay pride in Lawerence. *Boston Globe*.

Kneeland, P. (June 27, 1971). March, speeches mark Gay Pride Week. *Boston Globe*.

Krone, M. (September/October 2012). John Mitzel Isn't Going Anywhere. *Boston Spirit Magazine*.

Kyper, J. (July 2, 1972). Gay Pride Week—Towards a Community? *Boston After Dark*. https://historyproject.ome-ka.net/items/show/481

Lakshmanan, I.A. R. (March 20, 1995). S. Boston parade, already protesting gay group, bars veterans with AIDS. *Boston Globe*.

Langner, P. (November, 17, 1983). A Look at the Boston City Council; David Scondras. *Boston Globe*.

LaTronica, M. (July 2002). Please, burst my bubble. *Sojourner*.

Lavender Rhino, Inc. (1990). The Official Guide to Lesbian & Gay Pride Weeks in Boston. In: Lavender Rhino, Inc.

Ledgard, L. (June 19, 1983). 18,000 march in Hub for lesbian, gay pride. *Boston Globe*.

LePore, S. (December 31, 2023). Former Biden head of nuclear waste policy Sam Brinton ends 2023 a FREE person after being accused of stealing women's clothing from airport suitcases. *Daily Mail*. https://www.dailymail.co.uk/news/article-12915165/Sam -Brinton-Biden-official-free-2023.html

Leung, S. (June 13, 1996). Pride parade organizers vow to end lewdness. *Boston Globe*.

Levenson, M. (June 9, 2005). Patrick to march in Boston's gay parade; Reilly says he has prior commitment. *Boston Globe*.

Levenson, M. (September 30, 2006). Gay couple from R.I. win Mass. ruling; Superior Court Judge says longtime partners can marry. *Boston Globe*.

Levenson, M. (June 11, 2014). Democrats forced to choose: Pride or convention. *Boston Globe*.

Lewis, R., & Abraham, Y. (May 20, 2004). Senate votes to end 1913 law action is tied to gay marriages. *Boston Globe*.

Lewis, R. (May 16, 2005). Passage of marriage amendment in doubt. *Boston Globe*.

Lewis, R. (September 8, 2005). Reilly OK's 2008 initiative on ban of gay marriage. *Boston Globe*.

Liberate Boston Pride. (June 7, 2024). *A letter to Boston Pride for the People from 67 organizations* https://liberatebostonpride.wordpress.com

Loesch, C. (June 2, 2023). Boston Pride Returns After Controversy And COVID Forced A 3-Year Halt. *Patch.com*. https://patch.com/massachusetts/boston/boston-pride-returns-after-controversy-covid-forced-3-year-halt

Longcope, K. (June 1990). 70,000 rally for gay pride. *Boston Globe*.

Longcope, K. (June 9, 1991). Proud to march 90,000 turn out at parade to celebrate strides made by gays, lesbians. *Boston Globe*.

Lopez, R. (2019). *The Hub of the Gay Universe: An LGBTQ History of Boston, Provincetown, and Beyond*. Shawmut Peninsula Press.

"Love Is All You Need, 1970," Documented. (1970). In: Digital Collections of The History Project.

Macias, A. (June 15, 1986). Marchers express solidarity at Gay Pride parade: Gay Pride. *Boston Globe*.

Marcus, J. (June 10, 1981). Gays, lesbians vow march on mayoral aide's dismissal. *Boston Globe*.

Martinez, A. (June 11, 1995). Celebrating 25 years of Gay Pride. *Boston Globe*.

Mason, A. (June 10, 2016). Are Pride Parade's Corporate Ties Undermining Its Original Queer Activist Message? *WBUR*.

McCabe, K. (January 22, 2013). Obama stuns with call for gay rights. *Boston Globe*.

Meyer, M. (October 13, 2021). The Implosion of Boston's Pride Parade is a Sign of Things to Come. *Quillette*. https://quillette.com/2021/10/13/the-implosion-of-bostons-pride-parade-is-a-sign-of-things-to-come/

Migliori, L. (March 9, 1997). Boston Pride committee's guiding light: Sabrina Taylor. *InNewsweekly*.

Mitzel, J. (1970). Entry June 30, 1970. MS 1779, John Mitzel Papers, Series IV: Diaries 1961-2002 Box 31 Folder 830. In. Beinecke Rare Book & Manuscript Library at Yale University.

Mitzel, J. (1971a). Entry June 25, 1971. MS 1779, John Mitzel Papers, Series IV: Diaries 1961-2002 Box 31 Folder 832. In. Beinecke Rare Book & Manuscript Library at Yale University.

Mitzel, J. (1971b). The Lesson of Gay Pride Week: Beware the SWP. MS 1779, John Mitzel Papers, Series III: Professional Papers 1964-2013 Box 21 Folder 613. In. Beinecke Rare Book & Manuscript Library at Yale University.

Mitzel, J. (1972a). Entry May 7, 1972. MS 1779, John Mitzel Papers, Series IV: Diaries 1961-2002 Box 31 Folder 835. In. Beinecke Rare Book & Manuscript Library at Yale University.

Mitzel, J. (1972b). Entry May 30, 1972. MS 1779, John Mitzel Papers, Series IV: Diaries 1961-2002 Box 31 Folder 835. In. Beinecke Rare Book & Manuscript Library at Yale University.

Mitzel, J. (1972c). Entry June 25, 1972. MS 1779, John Mitzel Papers, Series IV: Diaries 1961-2002 Box 31 Folder 835. In. Beinecke Rare Book & Manuscript Library at Yale University.

Mitzel, J. (1973). Entry June 19, 1973. MS 1779, John Mitzel Papers, Series IV: Diaries 1961-2002 Box 31 Folder 837. In. Beinecke Rare Book & Manuscript Library at Yale University.

Mitzel, J. (1977a). Entry May 8, 1977. MS 1779, John Mitzel Papers, Series IV: Diaries 1961-2002 Box 32 Folder 849. In. Beinecke Rare Book & Manuscript Library at Yale University.

Mitzel, J. (1977b). Entry June 19, 1977. MS 1779, John Mitzel Papers, Series IV: Diaries 1961-2002 Box 32 Folder 849. In. Beinecke Rare Book & Manuscript Library at Yale University.

Mitzel, J. (1978a). Entry June 12, 1978. MS 1779, John Mitzel Papers, Series IV: Diaries 1961-2002 Box 32 Folder 852. In. Beinecke Rare Book & Manuscript Library at Yale University.

Mitzel, J. (1978b). Entry June 18, 1978. MS 1779, John Mitzel Papers, Series IV: Diaries 1961-2002 Box 32 Folder 852. In. Beinecke Rare Book & Manuscript Library at Yale University.

Mitzel, J. (1981). Entry June 24, 1981. MS 1779, John Mitzel Papers, Series IV: Diaries 1961-2002 Box 32 Folder 856. In. Beinecke Rare Book & Manuscript Library at Yale University.

Mitzel, J. (1982). Entry June 20, 1982. MS 1779, John Mitzel Papers, Series IV: Diaries 1961-2002 Box 32 Folder 857. In. Beinecke Rare Book & Manuscript Library at Yale University.

Mitzel, J. (1983). Entry May 21, 1983. MS 1779, John Mitzel Papers, Series IV: Diaries 1961-2002 Box 32 Folder 859. In. Beinecke Rare Book & Manuscript Library at Yale University.

Mitzel, J. (1984). Entry June 16, 1984. MS 1779, John Mitzel Papers, Series IV: Diaries 1961-2002 Box 32 Folder 860. In. Beinecke Rare Book & Manuscript Library at Yale University.

Mitzel, J. (1986). Entry June 9, 1986. MS 1779, John Mitzel Papers, Series IV: Diaries 1961-2002 Box 32 Folder 837. In. Beinecke Rare Book & Manuscript Library at Yale University.

Mitzel, J. (February 12, 2012). *Interview with John Mitzel* [Interview]. https://www.youtube.com/watch?v=2C0HAnuK3j4

Monroe, I. *About Irene Monroe*. Retrieved August 20, 2024 from https://www.irenemonroe.com/about/

Monroe, R. I. (June 20, 2018). What's happening to Pride? *Windy City Times*.

Monroe, R. I. (November 8, 2021). Why shut down Boston Pride? Racism is not the only reason for the closure. *Boston Spirit Magazine*.

Monroe, R. I. (June 16, 2022). Moving beyond Boston Pride with Pop-Up Pride on Boston Common. *Boston Spirit Magazine*. https://bostonspiritmagazine.com/2022/06/moving-beyond-boston-pride-with-pop-up-boston-pride-on-the-common/

Mont, J. (June 18-24, 1996). Pride and prejudice: Parade controversy creates rift among gay activists. *The Tab*. http://bostondykemarcharchive.weebly.com/uploads/7/0/2/5/7025237/tab_june_18_1996.pdf

Mont, J. (June 25-July 1, 1996). Clash takes place among gay leaders: Powerful political divisions bared in wake of parade. *The Tab*. http://bostondykemarcharchive.weebly.com/uploads/7/0/2/5/7025237/tab_july_1_1996.pdf

Morris, D. (June 13, 1981). Liaison position axed. *Gay Community News*.

Murphy, S., & Anand, G. (June 20, 1995). US decision is hailed in South Boston. *Boston Globe*.

Nangeroni, N. (1994). *Boston Pride Speech June 1994*. http://www.gendertalk.com/pride/

Nangeroni, N. (1998). *Boston Pride Speech June 1998*. http://www.gendertalk.com/pride-98/

Nealon, P. (November 11, 1993). S. Boston parade sponsors ordered to supply data. *Boston Globe*.

Neff, L. (June 25, 2002). Pride by many other names. *The Advocate*.

New Boston Pride Committee, I. (n.d.) Float Documentation for Participation in the Parade.

New Boston Pride Committee, I. *FY 2000 Form 990*.

New Boston Pride Committee, I. *FY 2002 Form 990*.

New Boston Pride Committee, I. *FY 2004 Form 990*.

New Boston Pride Committee, I. *FY 2008 Form 990*.

New Boston Pride Committee, I. *FY 2011 Form 990*.

New Boston Pride Committee, I. *FY 2012 Form 990*.

New Boston Pride Committee, I. *FY 2016 Form 990*.

New Boston Pride Committee, I. *FY 2015 Form 990*.

New Boston Pride Committee, I. *FY 2017 Form 990*.

New Boston Pride Committee, I. *FY 2020 Form 990*.

New Boston Pride Committee, I. (n.d.) Parade Vehicle Inspection Criteria.

New Boston Pride Committee, I. (2002). Welcome to Pride 2002. *2002 New England Pride Guide*.

New Boston Pride Committee, I. (2003). March Registration Form.

New Boston Pride Committee, I. (2006a). Boston Pride Newsletter. In (Vol. 1 Issue 1).

New Boston Pride Committee, I. (2006b). Boston Pride Newsletter. In (Vol. 1 Issue 2).

New Boston Pride Committee, I. (2006c). Boston Pride Parade 2006: Group Marshal Handbook.

New Boston Pride Committee, I. (June 7, 2006). *Statement of the Boston Pride Committee on Macy's Succumbing to Anti-Gay Sentiments* https://web.archive.org/web/20060619095938/http://www.boston-pride.org:80/MacysJune7.pdf

New Boston Pride Committee, I. (2007). *Amended and Restated By-Laws.*

New Boston Pride Committee, I. (2008). *By-Laws.*

New Boston Pride Committee, I. (2010). InterPride 30th Anniversary Annual General Meeting Preliminary Bid.

New Boston Pride Committee, I. (March 13, 2012). Boston to host InterPride's 2012 Annual World Conference, celebrating its 30th Anniversary. https://www.bostonpride.org/2012/03/boston-to-host-inter-prides-2012-annual-world-conference-celebrating-its-30th-an-niversary/

New Boston Pride Committee, I. (April 24, 2012). Boston Pride to Host InterPride Mid-Year Meeting. https://www.boston-pride.org/2012/04/boston-pride-to-host-inter-pride-mid-year-meeting/

New Boston Pride Committee, I. (May 31, 2012). DOMA declared unconstitutional. https://www.boston-pride.org/2012/05/doma-declared-unconstitutional/

New Boston Pride Committee, I. (May 1, 2013). Boston Pride announces first ever Pride Night @ Fenway Park! https://www.bostonpride.org/2013/05/boston-pride-an-nounces-first-ever-pride-night-fenway-park/

New Boston Pride Committee, I. (October 8, 2014). Boston Pride Launches Its Own Official Pride Guide in 2015. https://www.bostonpride.org/2014/10/boston-pride-launches-its-own-official-pride-guide-in-2015/

New Boston Pride Committee, I. (2015a). *2015 Boston Pride Gala*. Retrieved July 27, 2024 from http://web.archive.org/web/20150 609022709/https://www.bostonpride.org/gala/

New Boston Pride Committee, I. (2015b). Boston Pride Guide. In (Vol. 1): Sylvain Bruni.

New Boston Pride Committee, I. (May 12, 2015). Boston Pride Will Kick Off Pride Week and 45th Anniversary with First Ever Gala. https://www.boston-pride.org/2015/05/boston-pride-will-kick-off-pride-week-and-45th-anniversary-with-first-ever-gala/

New Boston Pride Committee, I. (June 16, 2015). Boston Pride Thanks Community for Successful 45th Annual Celebration. https://www.boston-pride.org/2015/06/boston-pride-thanks-community-for-successful-45th-annual-pride-week/

New Boston Pride Committee, I. (November 1, 2015). Introducing the Boston Pride Community Fund. https://www.bostonpride.org/2015/11/introducing-the-boston-pride-community-fund/

New Boston Pride Committee, I. (2016). Solidarity through Pride: With a commitment to community building, Boston Pride introduces two new programs. In. Boston Pride Guide 2016.

New Boston Pride Committee, I. (April 4, 2016). Boston Pride Statement Regarding Withdrawal of Parade Marshal. https://www.bostonpride.org/2016/04/boston-pride-statement-regarding-withdrawal-of-parade-marshal/

New Boston Pride Committee, I. (June 12, 2016). Boston Pride statement on the Orlando massacre. https://www.boston-pride.org/2016/06/boston-pride-statement-on-the-orlando-massacre/

New Boston Pride Committee, I. (July 1, 2016). A Look Back on Boston Pride Month 2016, Celebrations and Remembrances for the LGBT Community. https://www.boston-pride.org/2016/07/a-look-back-on-boston-pride-month-2016-celebrations-and-remembrances-for-the-lgbt-community/

New Boston Pride Committee, I. (June 29, 2017). Boston Pride attends World Pride 2017 in Madrid, Spain. https://www.bostonpride.org/2017/06/boston-pride-attends-world-pride-2017-in-madrid-spain/

New Boston Pride Committee, I. (December 5, 2017). Boston Pride VP Linda DeMarco elected co-president of InterPride. https://www.bostonpride.org/2017/12/boston-pride-vp-linda-demarco-elected-co-president-of-interpride/

New Boston Pride Committee, I. (2018). Boston Pride 2019 Partnership Packet.

New Boston Pride Committee, I. (December 18, 2018). Boston Pride Names Two New Board Members. https://www.boston-pride.org/2018/12/boston-pride-names-two-new-board-members/?ref=quillette.com

New Boston Pride Committee, I. (2019a). Boston Pride Guide. In (Vol. 5): Boston Pride.

New Boston Pride Committee, I. (2019b). 2019 Parade Line Up in Alpha Order.

New Boston Pride Committee, I. (2019c) *2019 Pride Marshals*. Retrieved June 18, 2024 from https://www.bostonpride.org/marshal/

New Boston Pride Committee, I. (August 26, 2019). *Statement by Boston Pride Regarding Straight Pride*. https://web.archive.org/web/20190902140533/https://www.bostonpride.org/2019/08/statement-by-boston-pride-regarding-straight-pride/

New Boston Pride Committee, I. (2020a). *#BlackLivesMatter*

New Boston Pride Committee, I. (2020b). *Boston Pride Reworked Statement on Black and Brown Police Violence*

New Boston Pride Committee, I. (2020c). *Letter to Our Community*

New Boston Pride Committee, I. (2020d). Trademark: Cease and Desist. In C. D. Henry Paquin, Jo Trigilio, Valerie Bee (Ed.).pride4thepeople.org.

New Boston Pride Committee, I. (2020e). Transformation Advisory Committee. In.

New England Gay Pride Week 1975: For Immediate Release. (June 13, 1975). In: The History Project Archives.

New England Gay Pride '76 Workshops. (1976). In: The History Project Archives.

Nilsson, C. (June 6, 2023). The Rise, Fall, and Hopeful Return of Boston's Pride Parade. *Boston Magazine*. https://www.bostonmagazine.com/news/2023/06/06/boston-pride-parade-back/

No Pinkwashing Boston. (June 21,2023). *Boston Rejects Zionist Pinkwashing* https://nopinkwashingboston.wordpress.com

No room on the stage? (July 1997). *Sojourner*.

Noble, E. (2021). *Stonewall Portraits: A Conversation with Elaine Noble* [Interview]. https://www.youtube.com/watch?v=8kqloL-WYj94

Obama, B. (January 21, 2013). *Inaugural Address by President Barack Obama* https://obamawhitehouse.archives.gov/the-press-of-fice/2013/01/21/inaugural-address-president-barack-obama

Obergefell v. Hodges, 651 (2015). https://www.supremecourt.gov/opinions/boundvolumes/576BV.pdf#page=696

O'Brien, E. (June 8, 1997). 100,000 march to celebrate Hub's Gay Pride event goes off with humor, teasing, community spirit. *Boston Globe*.

Outwords. *Outwords Archive: Nancy Nangeroni*. Retrieved September 20, 2024 from https://theoutwordsarchive.org/interview/nangeroni-nancy/

Pane, L. M. (June 17, 1984). 15,000 join Boston march for gay rights. *Boston Globe*.

Parade Plans Bring Criticism. (May 25, 1974). *Gay Community News*.

Pennington, J., Mulvihill, M., & Phelps, R. (May 25, 2023). The (R)Evolution of Boston Pride: How a grassroots group took over the Bay State's biggest LGBTQ+ event. *Boston Spirit Magazine*. https://bostonspiritmagazine.com/2023/05/the-revolution-of-boston-pride-how-a-grassroots-group-took-over-the-bay-states-biggest-lgbtq-event/

Phelps, R. (June 25, 2020). Boston Pride engages consultants to work on diversity and inclusion. *Boston Spirit Magazine*.

Phelps, R. (July 2, 2020). Tensions mount between Boston Pride and activists calling for board to resign. *Boston Spirit Magazine*.

Phelps, R. (July 9, 2021). After 50 years, Boston Pride to dissolve, announces its board of directors. *Boston Spirit Magazine*.

Pliner, E., & Taylor, S. (1998). Letter: Boston Pride 1998. In: The History Project Archives.

Police again out 'village' youths: Outbreak by 400 follows a near-riot over raid. (June 30,1969). *New York Times*.

Pride. (May 1999). *The Boston Phoenix.*

Pride 1996 Calendar of Events. (1996). In: The History Project Archives.

Pride Celebrations, Inc. (1985). Fifteen Years of Pride: The History and Purpose of Pride. In: Northeastern University Archives and Special Collections.

Program of Events for "the March" of Pride Fest '88. (1988). In: The History Project Archives.

Project, T. H. Pride 1971. (n.d.). In: The History Project Archives.

Project, T. H. Pride 1973. (n.d.). In: The History Project Archives.

Project, T. H. Pride 1974 with Notes. (n.d.). In: The History Project Archives.

Project, T. H. Pride 1975. (n.d.). In: The History Project Archives.

Project, T. H. Pride 1976 with Notes. (n.d.). In: The History Project Archives.

Project, T. H. Pride 1977. (n.d.). In: The History Project Archives.

Project, T. H. Pride 1978. (n.d.). In: The History Project Archives.

Project, T. H. Pride 1979. (n.d.). In: The History Project Archives.

Project, T. H. Pride 1982. (n.d.). In: The History Project Archives.

Project, T. H. Pride 1983. (n.d.). In: The History Project Archives.

Project, T. H. Pride 1984. (n.d.). In: The History Project Archives.

Project, T. H. Pride 1985. (n.d.). In: The History Project Archives.

Project, T. H. Pride 1986. (n.d.). In: The History Project Archives.

Project, T. H. Pride 1987. (n.d.). In: The History Project Archives.

Project, T. H. Pride 1991. (n.d.). In. The History Project Archives.

Project, T. H. Pride 1992. (n.d.). In. The History Project Archives.

Project, T. H. Pride 1994. (n.d.). In: The History Project Archives.

Project, T. H. Pride 1995. (n.d.). In: The History Project Archives.

Project, T. H. Pride 1996. (n.d.). In: The History Project Archives.

Puga, A. (June 20, 1995). high court says veterans can bar gays from parade Speech rights at issue in St. Patrick's event. *Boston Globe*.

Quinn, T., & Meiners, E. (July 29, 2015). Good cop? Bad cop? No cop! Queer resistance to policing. *Windy City Times*.

Reed, J. (June 3, 2004). Gay Pride heads to the chapel of love. *Boston Globe*.

Retro Pride Boston 1998: Calendar of Events. (1998). In: The History Project Archives.

Rezendes, M. (March 18, 1992). Flynn decries heckling of gays Vows to support new march bids. *Boston Globe*.

Rezendes, M. (March 14, 1994). Would-be marchers rap city Gay group grumbles at mayor's lack of contingency parade plan. *Boston Globe*.

Rhino Files Suit. (June 22, 1974). *Gay Community News*.

Rhino Wins Grant. (May 11, 1974). *Gay Community News*.

Ribadeniera, D. (October 7, 1997). Foster ruling stands up State placed boy in gay household. *Boston Globe*.

Ridinger, R. B. (Ed.). (2004). *Speaking for Our Lives: Historic Speeches and Rhetoric for Gay and Lesbian Rights 1892-2000*. Harrington Park Press.

Riemer, M., & Brown, L. (2019). *We Are Everywhere: Protest, Power, and Pride in the History of Queer Liberation*. Ten Speed Press.

Rights groups blast policy against gay foster parents. (May 28, 1985). *Boston Globe*.

Rimer, S. (December 4, 2019). Opening Doors: John Ward. *Bostonia*. https://www.bu.edu/articles/2019/a-career-spent-fighting-for-the-rights-of-lgbtq-individuals/#comments

Ring, T. (May14, 2022). Urvashi Vaid, Legendary Activist for LGBTQ+ Civil Rights, Dies at 63. *Advocate*. https://www.advocate.com/news/2022/5/14/legendary-activist-urvashi-vaid-dies-63

Rubin, E. (June 22, 1980). 5000, 'gay and proud,' march for their rights. *Boston Globe*.

Russell, J. (June 9, 2002). Parents, families celebrate gay pride. *Boston Globe*.

Salinas, S. (June 11, 2017). A celebration of Pride, with a tinge of mourning. *Boston Globe*.

Scott, G. *Gunner Scott*. Retrieved September 20, 2024 from https://about.me/gunnerscott

Secretary of the Commonwealth of Massachusetts. (1990). *Corporation Master Display: Lavender Rhino, Inc.*

Shanahan, M. (June 9, 2017). Boston Pride apologizes for Facebook post. *Boston Globe*.

Sipress, A. (June 20, 1982). Gays hold parade, rally in Boston. *Boston Globe*.

Sister Assaulted. (July 26, 1973).*Gay Community News*.

Society of Professional Journalists. (n.d.). *SPJ Code of Ethics*. https://www.spj.org/ethicscode.asp

Stanley, J. (June 29, 2021).Upcoming Film 'Playland' Serves As Memorial To Boston's Lost LGBTQ Spaces. *WBUR.org*. https://www.wbur.org/news/2021/06/29/boston-lost-lgbtq-spaces-playland-georden-west

Straw, J., Ford, B., & McShane, L. (April 17, 2013). Police narrow in on two suspects in Boston Marathon bombing. *The Daily News*.

Sudborough, S. (June 22, 2022). Rita Hester's murder and legacy are important to Boston, so she's getting a mural in Allston. *Boston.com*.

Sweeney, E. (June 26, 2019). Boston officials approve 'Straight Pride Parade' application; event to be held Aug 31. *Boston Globe*.

Taylor, J. (April 5, 1998). Permit request for gay march in Lawerence evokes debate. *Boston Globe*.

Tench, M. (June 15, 2003). Message-laden march puts politics, gay pride on parade. *Boston Globe.*

Tench, M. (May16, 2004). Wedding option energizes teenagers at youth pride rally. *Boston Globe.*

The Dyke March Committee (June 1996). *To the community*

The   Dyke   March   Committee   (1996).   *Post Bedgate Letter* http://bostondykemarcharchive.weebly.com/up-loads/7/0/2/5/7025237/post_bed_letter_n_poem_96.pdf

The gay agenda: Pride 2001. (June 7, 2001). *Boston Globe.*

The General Court of the Commonwealth of Mass-achusetts. (n.d.) *Section 34: Crime against na-ture.* https://malegislature.gov/Laws/GeneralLaws/PartIV/Ti-tleI/Chapter272/Section34

The General Court of the Commonwealth of Mass-achusetts. (n.d.) *Section 35: Unnatural and lascivi-ous acts.* https://malegislature.gov/Laws/GeneralLaws/PartIV/Ti-tleI/Chapter272/Section35

The History Project. *Home.* (n.d.). https://www.historyproject.org

The Network/La Red (February 2021). *Boycott Boston Pride: The Network/LA Red announces our boycott of Boston Pride* https://www.tnlr.org/en/boycott-boston-pride/

The Pride Committee, Inc. (1993). *1993 Form 990.* In. The History Project Archives.

The Rainbow Times (June 9, 2018). Queer & Trans PoC Elevate Concerns of Systemic Racism at Boston Pride Parade. *The Rainbow   Times.* https://www.therainbowtimesmass.com/queer-trans-poc-ele-vate-concerns-of-systemic-racism-at-boston-pride-pa-rade/?ref=quillette.com

The Rainbow Times. (July 9, 2021). Boston Pride dissolves after pressure. *The Rainbow Times.*

Thorstad, D. (Ed.). (1976). *Gay Liberation and Socialism: Documents From the Discussions on Gay Liberation Inside the Socialist Workers Party (1970-1973).*

Tobin, T. (April 28, 2002). Bankruptcy, ill will plague Bryant. *St. Petersburg Times.*

Trans Resistance MA. *About the Resistance.* Retrieved August 22, 2024 from https://www.transresistancema.com/about

Trigilio, J. (n.d.). *Political Context: Controversy over scheduled Bitch performance at the 2007 Dyke March* [Interview]. http://bostondykemarcharchive.weebly.com/uploads/7/0/2/5/7025237/1._bitch_political_context.pdf

Trigilio, J. (2022). *Interview* [Interview].

Ulloa, J. (June 14, 2009). Pride Parade mourns loss of longtime leader. *Boston Globe.*

Valencia, M. (December 8, 2012). High court takes on gay marriage case. *Boston Globe.*

Vennochi, J. (June 14, 2007). Marriage debate is a test of Patrick's power. *Boston Globe.*

Walker, A. (January 7, 1993). Veterans ask court to halt gays' hearing on parade. *Boston Globe.*

Wang, V., & Allen, E. (June 11, 2016). Boston's Pride Parade was a celebration, and a statement. *Boston Globe.*

Wangsness, L. (June 8, 2007). Patrick to join march for gay pride. *Boston Globe.*

Weir, J. (August 23, 1994). Mad about the boys: What is the story behind NAMBLA? Our writer visits the boy lovers' summer convention. *Advocate.*

Witcher, G. (June 8, 1984). 400 homosexuals rally, mark gay pride week in Boston. *Boston Globe*.

Wong, D. S. (February 20, 1993). Gays win OK to join parade Sponsors ordered to lift St. Pat's ban. *Boston Globe*.

Woolhouse, M. (June 13, 2010). Boston's gay pride parade goes marching through the rain. *Boston Globe*.

Yee, V. (June 12, 2011). Rain doesn't dampen pride parade. *Boston Globe*.

@jacques_cabaret. (June 8, 2024). *We at Jacques would like to publicly apologize for leaving af*ck*ng bus in the middle of the parade. We intended to ride it to the finishline, but it broke down and we evacuated like it was d*mn Titanic. We hope thecity of Boston can forgive us in time, but in the meantime, please come to ourshows today at 3pm, 7pm, and 10pm. Happy Pride.* X.

Index

H

O

P

U

U2, 98

U.S. Association of Prides, 196

UMass Boston, 27

Unitarian Universalists, 105

United Front of Gay Organizations in Boston, 9. *See also Travis, Diane; Kennedy, Magorah; Kaplan, Dana; McMurray, Laura*

United Fruit Co, 53

United States Department of Justice, 132

United States Supreme Court, 3, 59, 74–75, 77–78, 101–103, 125, 132. *See also St. Patrick's Day Parade*

Unity Pride, 89

UpStairs Lounge, 21. *See also New Orleans, LA*

V

Vaid, Urvashi, 62

Vaughn, Athena, 159

Viva, Eli, 140

W

Walsh, Marty, 145

Ward, John, 38, 74–75, 117. *See also GLBTQ Legal Advocates & Defenders (GLAD); St. Patrick's Day Parade*

Warren, Elizabeth, 123, 143

Washington, DC, 62

Wasserman, Michael, 45–46

Watertown, MA, 125